Another Order

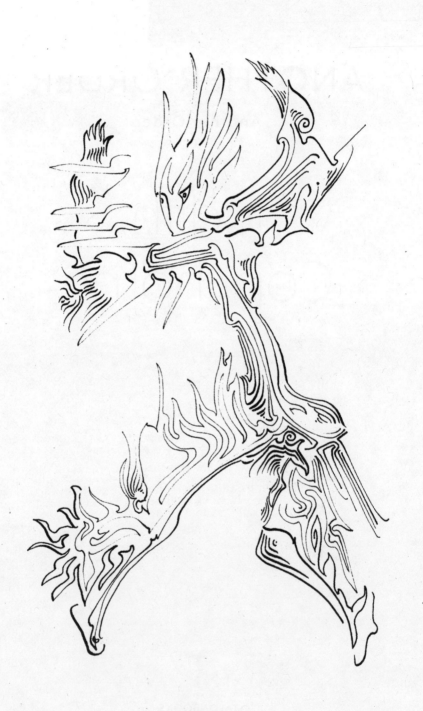

ANOTHER ORDER

Judith Copithorne

SELECTED WORKS

EDITED WITH AN INTRODUCTION
BY ERIC SCHMALTZ

TALONBOOKS

Talonbooks
9259 Shaughnessy Street, Vancouver, British Columbia, Canada v6p 6rw4
talonbooks.com

Talonbooks is located on xʷməθkʷəy̓əm, Sḵwx̱wú7mesh, and səlilwətaɬ Lands.

First printing: 2023

Typeset in Arno
Printed and bound in Canada on 100% post-consumer recycled paper

Interior and cover design by Leslie Smith
Cover illustration by Judith Copithorne
Image on p. ii by Judith Copithorne, *Release*, 1969
Image on p. 352 by Judith Copithorne, *Redro*, 2006

Talonbooks acknowledges the financial support of the Canada Council for the
Arts, the Government of Canada through the Canada Book Fund, and the Province
of British Columbia through the British Columbia Arts Council and the Book
Publishing Tax Credit.

Library and Archives Canada Cataloguing in Publication

Title: Another order : selected works / Judith Copithorne ; edited with an
introduction by Eric Schmaltz.
Other titles: Works. Selections
Names: Copithorne, Judith, author. | Schmaltz, Eric, 1988- editor.
Description: Includes bibliographical references.
Identifiers: Canadiana 20230455956 | ISBN 9781772015539 (softcover)
Classification: LCC PS8555.O59296 A6 2023 | DDC C811/.54—dc23

THERE'S ANOTHER ORDER
TO THINGS
IN WHICH WE
PERHAPS UNKNOWINGLY
LIVE

—JUDITH COPITHORNE
RELEASE (1969)

Introduction

Eric Schmaltz

Words will rush to us
   like a river of stars
The form will form us and formed
   we will form

—Judith Copithorne, "Affirmative Poem"

Another Order: Selected Works brings together a robust selection of Judith Copithorne's writing and hybrid publications drawn from over fifty years of her practice. Alongside selections of recent digital-born visual poetry representative of her ongoing aesthetic transformations, it collects her early poem-drawings and hybrid texts such as *Meandering* (1967) and *Rain* (1969), collections of stanzaic poetry such as *Until Now* (1971) and *A Light Character* (1985), sequenced short fiction such as *Heart's Tide* (1972), personal essays, and more that have been entrusted to small presses and privately published in limited-edition runs, many of which are long out of print. As an extensive collection of her publications, *Another Order* represents what Lorna Brown describes as Copithorne's "embodied approach to text" that maintains resolute "physicality and immersive concentration, fully open to new influences and challenges" whether the text is written, drawn, typed, or digitally created.[1] When reflecting on the importance of the writer's openness to media and aesthetic experimentation, Copithorne confesses that writing is most interesting to her "when it is surprising, unexpected, & outside the bounds."[2] Being "outside the bounds" is an apt description of Copithorne's artistic practice, since it stridently resists categorization and shatters the conventions that often make genre, media, and mode recognizable to readers. Throughout her life and work, Copithorne has consistently sought to manifest another order for writing and art-making that opens expressive possibilities for herself and the broader literary culture.

Describing the versatility of her technical prowess in two words, Copithorne identifies herself as an "intermedia worker," an identity that nods to *intermedia* – a term often used in the 1960s and 1970s and offered by Fluxus artist Dick Higgins – to describe what might also be approximately referred to as interdisciplinary and cross-media work. For Higgins, however, the term describes practices that are "between media,"[3] that draw multiple, disparate mediums into a singular context. Thus intermedia artistic practices are tantamount to alchemy, involving undertakings of transformation, movement, and combination across the arts. Copithorne's writing embodies these principles and dynamically moves between illustration, sketching, calligraphy, and typewriting while bringing together poetry, visual art, comics, life writing, and more to provide evidence that her tireless fusing of technique, mode, and genre locates her among the vanguard of her time. The title "intermedia worker" also characterizes Copithorne's position within Vancouver's creative community and her commitment to the proliferation of artistic practices while supporting the work of other women. Carole Itter has described Copithorne as one of the "astounding young women" of Vancouver's scene, "who insisted that their statements be heard and that they could be artists."[4] In the heyday of the counterculture movement, Copithorne contributed to Vancouver's artist-run venues the Sound Gallery and Motion Studio, where she danced as part of Helen Goodwin's

TheCo group, and she was an active member of Intermedia, an artist-run space dedicated to the collaborative exploration of emergent media by visual artists, filmmakers, musicians, poets, and more. She contributed to these vital hubs as an artist, writer, and dancer and, at times, also helped with the maintenance of these spaces – sanding floors, filling holes, painting walls, and contributing to event and exhibition planning. Painter Gregg Simpson recalls that during the 1960s and 1970s Copithorne, "like her colleague Maxine Gadd, broke the grip of the paternalistic elites and opened the door for later poets like Mona Fertig and others to continue the movement towards greater inclusion in the local scene, including being the driving force behind many small-press publications and readings."[5] Copithorne is a vital inspiration for writers and artists of many identities today.

Despite being a pioneer of mid twentieth-century intermedia art and writing in Canada, Copithorne's work has been distressingly underrecognized in avant-garde and multimedia literary circles. She has not enjoyed, for example, the same cultural currency as other intermedia artists of her generation – notably friends such as bill bissett and bpNichol, who published her and whom Copithorne published in her magazine *Returning*. Her elision from Canadian cultural discourse may be partially, albeit generously, understood as the result of the contingent materiality of her publications – often produced by small and micro-presses in limited-edition runs, and many of these presses no longer exist to bolster her work. Yet, and more poignantly, Copithorne has demonstrated a keen awareness of her marginalized position within Canadian cultural discourse and community, especially as a woman and intermedia poet. Paraphrasing a conversation she had with Copithorne, media scholar Lori Emerson writes on her blog that Copithorne "speculates" that "back in those days [the 1960s], dirty concrete [poetry] was considered pretty 'out there' and women were already having a hard enough time getting noticed for less 'out there' work."[6] While bissett's and Nichol's proximities to the centre of Canadian literary power are marginal when compared to prominent writers of the same generation such as Margaret Atwood or Michael Ondaatje, they have been to some degree acknowledged by the Canadian literati by awards and recognitions, anthologies, edited collections, and academic studies. Copithorne's writing, however, is doubly "outside the bounds" since her poetry circulates within the provisional networks of avant-garde literary production and has been often excluded on account of gendered biases.

The publication of *Another Order* marks an overdue return to Copithorne's writing and art. In *Judith: Women Making Visual Poetry* (2021) – an anthology that celebrates Copithorne with its title – poet Amanda Earl remarks that "When few women were being recognized for anything, and especially not for their visual poetry, Judith was paving the way for me and other women."[7] *Another Order* is an opportunity for readers to return to and survey the passage that Copithorne opened and enjoy her many contributions to a diversity of expressive forms. "Returning" is a word central to Copithorne's life and lexicon. Beginning in 1965, she uses it as the moniker for her small press that sporadically issues exquisitely designed chapbooks and pamphlets. Some of the material details that characterize her publications range from sheet and card covers bound with meticulous Japanese stitching to digitally printed publications that intimate careful attention to image and paper quality. This notion of "returning" to Copithorne's body of work is particularly momentous, since *Returning* is also the name of her small press magazine, which featured the work of other writers and artists such as Daphne Marlatt, bill bissett, George Bowering, bpNichol, Mona Fertig, Maxine Gadd, Carole Itter, Gladys Hindmarch, and others. In one sense, writing and art have been constants in Copithorne's life; they are practices to which – following the patterns of moon cycles, tides, and seasonal transitions that prominently feature in her work – she has always returned. However, "returning" also identifies her desire to give back to her communities, to return work marked by her spirited generosity and singular vision.

Surprising Writing: Poem-Drawings and Hybrid Work

As this collection illustrates, Copithorne's creative practice is demonstrative of undeniable aesthetic diversity, yet in literary circles she is most often regarded as a pioneer of concrete and visual poetry in Canada. She has referred to this kind of work as "poem-drawings" to underscore the centrality of dextrous methods such as drawing, sketching, calligraphy, and handwriting to her repertoire. Regardless of whether they are hand drawn, typewritten, or digital, visual and concrete poetry are related forms that are exemplary manifestations of intermedia for the way they often bring together visual and linguistic modes of expression. In many scholarly accounts, Copithorne is recognized as a staple figure among Vancouver's so-called Downtown Poets – a designation advanced by the University of British Columbia's Warren Tallman, an American expatriate professor and literary critic, who distinguished active poetic factions in Vancouver in the 1960s. In other words, her writing was unlike the poetry cultivated by UBC's TISH poets George Bowering, Frank Davey, David Dawson, Lionel Kearns, Jamie Reid, and Fred Wah, and the slightly younger cohort of Robert Hogg, Daphne Marlatt, Dan McLeod, and David Cull – many of whom were deeply influenced by American poets who visited the university such as Robert Duncan and Charles Olson. In Tallman's distinction, the so-called Downtown Poets – Copithorne, bissett, Gadd, and others – embraced bohemian social life and counterculture politics and could be identified as intermedia writers because of their interest in moving across or combining expressive forms. The combination of their bohemianism, distrust of academia, and inclination towards literary experimentation separated these writers from the TISH group. They were a radical force in Vancouver committed to developing a lively alternative art scene that brought poetry into conversation with music, dance, painting, film, drawing, architecture, and more. Poetry that explored and experimented with language as a visual medium featured strongly within this node of Vancouver's community, and Copithorne is one of its indispensable figures.

Early in her career, Copithorne was regularly featured in premier publications for formally inventive poetries, such as Nichol's mimeographed publications *grOnk* and *Ganglia*; Nichol later edited Copithorne's book of stanzaic poetry *A Light Character* for Coach House Press. bissett featured forty-eight of her works across eleven issues of *blewointment* between 1963 and 1973. In fact, in the September 1964 issue, Copithorne published two distinctive poem-drawings, reflective of her inclination towards an intermedia practice. Placing cursive text alongside a line drawing of a woman, Copithorne writes,

This
was
drawn
last year
yet until I dreamed of it
this afternoon when
I laid with you
in the sun
I never knew what I had done[8]

These kinds of text and image intermixtures were the first of their ilk to be published in *blewointment* and, as Gregory Betts suggests, prophetic of what "would come to proliferate in the magazine and then throughout the city and beyond."[9] It could be said that the prophecy Copithorne's poem foretells is the coming wave of avant-garde art and intermedia work that would envelop Vancouver and elsewhere in Canada. These poems are a major landmark for a specific strain of avant-garde practice invested in blurring writing with other media, a practice that in Canada began in the 1960s and continues in the hybrid and intergenre work of writers today.

In Vancouver in the 1960s, when this kind of work enjoyed a notable surge of interest and activity, Copithorne was featured in several major exhibitions, including the *Concrete Poetry Festival: An Exhibition in Four Parts* at the Fine Arts Gallery at the University of British Columbia (March 28 to April 19, 1969) and *Microprosophus*, an international exhibition of visual poetry curated by poet David UU at Vancouver's Avelles Gallery in September 1971 (which was also exhibited elsewhere on other occasions). These were significant events for concrete and visual poetry in Vancouver – and Canada – not only for the high-calibre work they featured but for the international roster of poets and artists they attracted. Though centred around Vancouver poets such as bissett and Copithorne, *Microprosophus*, for example, featured over thirty contributors from eleven different countries. UBC's *Concrete Poetry Festival: An Exhibition in Four Parts* also featured numerous Vancouver poets alongside an international cast featuring Yoko Ono 小野 洋子 (Japan/USA), Eugen Gomringer (Bolivia/Germany), Dom Sylvester Houédard (England), Bob Cobbing (England), Ian Hamilton Finlay (Scotland), Seiichi Nikunii 新国誠一 (Japan), and others. Copithorne's work is unquestionably worthy of these esteemed international coteries since, as Caroline Bayard puts it, her word and image combinations have a "graphic sophistication and elegance one is not normally accustomed to in Canada."[10] Thus it should be no surprise that her concrete poetry was also included in representative anthologies of that time: John Robert Colombo's *New Direction in Canadian Poetry* (1971), Nichol's *The Cosmic Chef* (1970), *Four Parts Sand* (1972), and bissett's *THE LAST BLEWOINTMENT ANTHOLOGY VOLUME 1* (1985). Decades later, Copithorne maintains a strong presence on the scene with work featured in exhibitions such as 1994's *The Language Show* at A Space in Toronto, 2011's group show *The Bird is the Word* at the Niagara Artists Centre in St. Catharines, Ontario, and the travelling group show *Concrete Is Porous*, which touched down across Canada in Toronto, Ottawa, Windsor, and Victoria in 2018 through to 2020. Her work has been recently anthologized in *The Last Vispo*

Anthology: Visual Poetry 1998–2008 (2012) and *Judith: Women Making Visual Poetry* (2021), the latter honouring her dedication to exploring the intersection of word and image by using her first name in its title.

Copithorne's interest in the interplay between word and image preceded the West Coast's frenzied excitement in the 1960s; notable influences contextualize her visual and concrete poetry collected here. In an interview with poet Gary Barwin, she recalls images from *The Book of Kells* "that relatives sent at Christmas" to be one of her early points of reference[11] – that is, the ninth-century illuminated manuscript containing four Gospels of the New Testament alongside extravagantly designed and coloured decoration and traditional Christian iconography. She also recalls that as a young person she frequently read the *New Statesman,* a British magazine to which her parents subscribed known for its left-wing views and socially progressive attitude – playwright George Bernard Shaw was among its founding directors. Copithorne recalls flipping through the magazine to the back pages, where she read news about recent publications by the likes of Gertrude Stein and exhibitions by renowned modernist painters. Both printed forms – where the interplay of imagery and language is central to the expression of ideas – certainly informed Copithorne's artistic purview in more than one way. In the case of the *New Statesman,* she gained familiarity with groundbreaking twentieth century European artists and writers, and generally, by absorbing both kinds of works, she registered the artistic, social, and political power embedded in cultivating meaningful relationships between word and image.

These influences naturally led Copithorne to a fascination with literary figures such as Romantic poet William Blake and his enigmatic illuminated books *Songs of Innocence* (1789) and *Songs of Experience* (1794), wherein visionary lyrics are accompanied by illustrations of death, destruction, light, and liberation. In *The Cosmic Chef,* Nichol regards Copithorne as "One of the few clear successors to the tradition William Blake founded,"[12] identifying the mystical quality of her poetry that combines word and image in ways similar to Blake's. In her 1973 book *Arrangements*, for example, her poetry intermingles with her visions of home life, animals, and companions, elevating her everyday environment to a status worthy of sustained attention and artifice. The final page of *Arrangements*, for example, is a still-life illustration of a plant, a book of poems by Emily Dickinson, and two framed pictures which is accompanied by a short, handwritten poem:

> April 19
> What we have done then,
> was the best we could do.
> There should be more …
> will be
> since all things change,
> and continue, also.[13]

By taking the words and image together, the speaker offers a profound appreciation for the nature of sight and seemingly mundane objects. With the poem, the speaker acknowledges that this piece captures a static, singular arrangement of these objects among the many transformations they will endure beyond this illustrated moment. In works like these, Copithorne demonstrates an acute sensitivity to the forceful interplay between human physicality and experience with the materials of the everyday – their shared capacity to influence and shape and respond to one another. What seem like inanimate objects to some have vital animism to Copithorne, a spiritual quality reminiscent of Blake's personal poetic mythology. Concern for the powerful interplay between forces – whether they are human and nonhuman, image and language, spirit and material – strongly features in the works collected here.

Alongside Blake, Copithorne identifies visual art influences closer to her own milieu, highlighting 1961 as the year she encountered works by artist, poet, and inventor Brion Gysin and artist Henri Michaux at San Francisco's infamous City Light Books – a crucial West Coast hub for the American Beats and their brand of bohemianism and anti-authoritarian politics. Gysin and Michaux, aesthetically diverse practitioners in their own right, are predecessors to what in the 1990s came to be known as asemic writing. Peter Schwenger broadly defines asemic writing as "writing that does not attempt to communicate any message other than its own nature as writing."[14] Put differently, poet Tim Gaze, who is credited for his part in coining the term, explains that asemic writing is "anything which looks like writing, but in which the person viewing can't read any words."[15] Asemic writing occupies a liminal space between drawing and writing, wherein the marks upon the page may prompt the viewer to seek a recognizable language, but find nothing more than the mark as a material presence. Michaux's *Mouvements* (1951) are notable works representative of this kind of artistry; each of them comprises a series of markings that look language-like but contain no actual semantic content. Explaining his approach to works such as these, Michaux writes, "I wanted to draw moments that, end to end, make up life, to make visible the interior sentence, the sentence without words, the cord that unrolls itself indefinitely, sinuously, and deep within accompanies everything that presents itself, outside as well as inside."[16] Michaux's *Mouvements* bears a striking resemblance to Copithorne's emotive chapbook *Rain* (1969), a suite of poems wherein she shifts between handwritten semantic text and asemic marks to capture the feelings of a pained speaker lamenting a lost lover. In *Rain*, the hand-drawn elements capture the feeling body in action. We can see the body where she pressed, pulled, and lifted her pen off the page, sometimes heavy with an inky intensity and sometimes with wispy softness. These asemic elements underscore the speaker's unspeakable turmoil, expressing those feelings not only in words but also, like a dancer, in the gestures of the body moving across the surface of the page. Motion, pressure, and gesture – no matter how small – feature strongly throughout Copithorne's oeuvre as part of her personal visual language. While Schwenger may suggest that asemic writing "does not attempt to communicate any message,"[17] we can see how Copithorne's asemic writing carries the whole of her body and all its capacity for being in the world – her affect and, importantly, her subjectivity. It is an embodied practice, a means of drawing the movements of a body in space, of a body feeling deeply and in tune with the surfaces for mark-making.

Given this contextualization of Copithorne's visual and concrete poetry, it is clear that she is writing within a rich lineage of artists and writers – ranging from the ancients to moderns – but her combinations of word and image are most compelling for the intervention she makes into these traditions. As I have argued elsewhere, Copithorne's work embodies scholar Barbara Godard's notion of the "ex-centrique" writer.[18] That is, in Godard's usage of the term, a woman who has been excluded from the centres of literary power and who explores the potential of writing that could be described with words such as "diffused, disordered, circular, multiple, unpredictable, unstructured, and uncensored."[19] Copithorne seized on the powers of these descriptors at some of the earliest stages of her practice, as evidenced by the title of her second collection of poetry – but her first hand-drawn concrete poetry collection – *Meandering*, a title that invokes disorder, diffusion, and unpredictability. These works are labyrinthine, combining poetic language and abstract line work. The reader's eye must carefully discern Copithorne's flowing cursive language from her pirouetting lines that resist the linearity of readerly convention. As in much of Copithorne's early hand-drawn work, the reader's eyes are forced to meander across the page just as Copithorne's hand did with the pen, rotating the page, following a line of text until it terminates, only to jump to another starting point and follow it until it ends. These texts can be read from left to right, right to left, up and down, down and up, clockwise and counter-clockwise, beginning and ending wherever the reader pleases. Such inventions liberate the reader from Western readerly conventions but also create numerous alternative sequences that do not present a "set text but a range of possible texts depending on the eye's whim."[20] Thus Copithorne's visual and concrete poetry often unsettles conventional interpretive practices for readers and critics. The diffuse and disordered lines in texts like

Meandering are, like her asemic work, markings of the body in time and space, moving in tandem with her language. But, given their disruptive quality, they can also be described in theorist Sianne Ngai's words as "inarticulate mark[s]" that "deliberately interfere with close reading, a practice based on the principle that what is at stake in every textual encounter is a hidden or buried object, a concept of symbolic meaning that can be discovered by the reader only if she or he [or they] reads 'deeply' enough."[21] Poet Derek Beaulieu takes up this concept in *fractal economies* to describe a vast array of concrete and visual poetries; however, given the gendered context within which Copithorne sees her work, the power of her disruption of and purposeful swerve from processes of signification is even more significant.[22]

The 2010s saw a celebratory return to disruptive, intermedia poetry, especially typewritten visual and concrete poetry from the 1960s and 1970s, as represented in 2014's *Typewriter Art: A Modern Anthology,* edited by Barrie Tullett, and 2015's *The Art of Typewriting,* edited by avid collectors and supporters Ruth Sackner and Marvin Sackner. Both astounding anthologies prominently feature writers and artists who purposefully turned the typewriter away from its conventional, communicative purposes in acts that French avant-gardists L'Internationale situationniste might recognize as *détournement.* Works in Tullet's anthology such as those by the aforementioned monk Houédard – regarded as "the single most important figure in the history of typewriter art"[23] – or those by British Canadian poet Steve McCaffery push the typewriter's utilitarian functionality to extremes, presenting complex and often excessively layered typewritten designs that use letters and punctuation marks not to necessarily communicate a message, but instead to create "inarticulate mark[s]" that challenge signification processes.[24] In many ways, artists like McCaffery and Houédard are kindred spirits for Copithorne, since they too seek to disrupt semantic transmission by creating works that signify otherwise, that reach towards, as McCaffery might call it, "writing outside writing."[25] Copithorne's poem-drawings similarly unsettle textual processes by creating marks that resist signifying processes and reach outside of the literary economy of conventional meaning-making.

Given the prominence of the typewriter as the tool of choice for many concrete poets in the 1960s and 1970s, Copithorne's hand-drawn work stands out for its rejection of the typewriter, especially given the connotations it bears at the intersection of gender and labour. As Darren Wershler explains, criticism regarding the typewriter has exaggerated its oft-cited status as an apparatus that led to the liberation of women's labour. This is a claim, he notes, that is overturned by the image of the "Typewriter Girl," a title that infantilizes women workers who were hired as secretaries, paid significantly lower wages than men, and "rarely if ever enter the management stream."[26] The typewriter, then, for some may be seen as a device of liberation, but it also is reflective of demands on women to give themselves over to the machinic exigencies of corporate life without appropriate compensation and to dedicate their minds and bodies to the steady functioning of a predominantly masculine workplace. Copithorne's early hand-drawn visual and concrete poetry rejects the typewriter as a tool for poetic expression, a tool that many men at the time détourned for their own radical agenda. Frustration with gendered inequality and stereotypes features prominently in Copithorne's work – visual and otherwise. In *Release*, for example, she expresses dissatisfaction with conformism and gendered stereotypes of women; she writes, "Little girl you've become / a fuss budget / a worry wart / a harried / house wife / Let it all go   Let it / all go   Let go / fly free."[27] This language, frequently used by men, infantilizes and dehumanizes women. In response, the poem encourages the implied reader to "Let go" and to "fly free," anticipating Godard's theorization of the "ex-centrique" that empowers women artists to liberate women from the status of the subordinated other. While the hand-drawn approach that characterized much of her work in the 1960s and 1970s necessarily displaces her from the celebratory anthologies of typewriter art, it forces us to reckon with Copithorne's inimitable vision and her execution of it. It gives presence to her body and gendered identity on the page in a way that typewriters understandably cannot. Her hand-drawn work creates an aesthetic intimacy and textuality that attends to depths of feeling, thought, and experience that language cannot adequately express, while offering a powerful means for articulating her body and subjectivity as worthy of artifice in a culture that did not see it as such.

It would be a fallacy to claim that Copithorne totally resisted the typewriter as a tool for her "embodied approach to text,"[28] however. She was conscious of the medium's power to shape expression, and she did after all compose on the typewriter – notably *Heart's Tide* (1972), a semi-fictional sequence that swirls around ideas related to gender, embodiment, desire, and sexuality. The typewriter is mentioned at various points by the narrator, who types "while sitting in a lotus position," but admits that "This world of machines often stymies me," a moment that perhaps echoes Copithorne's actual relationship to the typewriter during that period. Decades later, though, Copithorne composed a suite of typewritten and hand-drawn poems entitled *Horizon* (1992), which was first published as a slim stack of Xeroxed pages bound by a single staple. This latter text, included in this volume, marks a transformation in Copithorne's writing and provides evidence of her interest in other media as mark-making devices. These poems appear long after the peak of typewriter-based concrete poetry in the 1960s and 1970s, but with phrases such as "falling behind" and "out of touch" and on a later page "love lost"[29] that have a lament-like quality. Considering that *Horizon* appears long after the typewriter's heyday, it is difficult not to read these poems as Copithorne's retrospective commentary on that moment. Given the language noted above, and that *Horizon* was only a fleeting experiment with the typewriter, these poems point to disappointment with a medium that launched the literary careers of many who continue to dominate the field while others have been left behind.

Copithorne pushed her concrete poetry still further beyond the typed and hand drawn to the digital realm, wherein she has composed hundreds of colourful combinations of text and image. Her more recent publications collected here, *Brackets & Boundaries {Concrete & Other Accretions}* (2011) and *Phases / Phrases* (2019), are representative of this embrace of digital methods that sustained her interest for much longer than the typewriter would.[30] While working with the computer may seem like a departure from her embodied poem-drawings, it should be remembered that the word "digital" comes from the Latin word *digitalis*, meaning "measuring a finger's breadth" and "relating to the finger."[31] Thus we should be reminded that the oft-perceived division between bodies and computer technologies is ill-conceived and that computers, in some cases, can register the body on the screen as effectively as the hand on the page. In fact, the back-cover copy for *Phases / Phrases* emphasizes that despite Copithorne's leaps between media "there is always her distinctive *touch*"[32] (my emphasis). In these collections, the poems maintain the signature characteristics of her earlier work – mixing words and images together with lines that meander, that are disordered, layered, and multidirectional, relying on a computer program's assortment of textures, strokes, and colours to capture the "relativity / of space, of / time, of light, emotions. / sensations, of ideas, of / experience, of colour."[33] Though the computer requires swipes, clicks, and taps that are unlike typical gestures of the pen or brush, it still allows her to bend words and phrases as in "19.4.11 fail safe," where many of the words – "splatter," "splotch," "stop," for example – contort in ways that recall her language's visual flexibility in *Meandering*. Likewise, digital composition programs often offer a wider array of simulated brush types, which we can see her exploring across the pages of these collections. Yet digital devices also allow Copithorne to push beyond the realism that digital tools can replicate and explore more whimsical and strange variations, thus keeping in step with her work that seeks to push boundaries and be "outside the bounds." Concluding her chapbook of digital concrete poetry and hybrid works, *Brackets & Boundaries {concrete & other accretions}*, Copithorne reflects on what it means to have boundaries and to be boundaryless. "Throughout human history," she remarks, "some boundaries have been fluid or entirely mutable & yet other boundaries have been, & continue to be, militarily maintained by means of surveillance & armaments. & those in power continue to attempt to destroy any boundaries but their own."[34] As an intermedia worker, Copithorne is hardly interested in maintaining boundaries that would confine her practice and only seeks to destroy boundaries that hinder creative exploration across contexts or result in the exclusion of others, like the boundaries that posed obstacles for women artists and writers in her community.

Beyond Concrete: Underground Comics and Graphic Antinarratives

Readers of this book will notice that Copithorne's visual writing pushes "beyond the bounds" of porous categories such as concrete and visual poetry and, in some cases, slants towards other genres, including the closely related field of comics. *Arrangements*, for example, is a text wherein verbal language is sometimes presented with "juxtaposed pictorial and other images in a deliberate sequence,"[35] a central feature that, according to Scott McCloud, distinguishes the comic as an art form. The speech bubble, another common feature in comics, appears on a few pages – notably on one comic-adjacent page thematizing communication: "Don't you always talk to whoever listens?" says one character.[36] Likewise, another hand-drawn collection, *Miss Tree's Pillow Book* (1971), adopts a similar formal feature with a panel sequence that depicts an unnamed character drifting off to sleep, to awake in an interstitial world occupied by a dream creature: "I'm the dream which seizes you in the dead of night," it says before it whisks her away and deposits her in "the land of fantasy." There the protagonist meets another nameless figure who encourages her to speak. "I have nothing to say," says the protagonist, to which the dream figure responds, "Sure you have."[37] The final panel is tinged with irony as the protagonist wonders aloud if she has anything to say at all. The implications of this comic are significant. On the one hand, we have a female protagonist who, through her dream travel, muses about her expressive powers. Notably, Copithorne draws this comic during a time, as discussed above, when women's voices were too often eclipsed by a dominant patriarchal culture, especially in Canadian poetry. On the other hand, the character's difficulty in finding words worth expressing also points to a recurrent motif in Copithorne's oeuvre regarding the limits of language – its inability to capture the full, true range of human experience. On a more general level, it provokes us to compare Copithorne's hand-drawn, intermedia works to comics. If we take scholar Robert Harvey's definition of comics as a form that emphasizes the blend of "word and image" to "achieve a meaning that neither conveys alone without the other"[38] then we might, in a generous interpretation of this definition, approximate some of Copithorne's graphic work to the field of comics and graphic narratives.

While Copithorne would not recognize these genres as directly influential on her art and writing, the resonances between her hybrid work and similar graphic explorations happening concurrently in Canada are noteworthy, especially given the recent resurgent interest in British Canadian artist and illustrator Martin Vaughn-James. Vaughan-James's experimental "visual novels," including his visual novel *The Cage* (originally published by Coach House Press in 1975), were concurrently published with Copithorne's 1970s graphic publications. In *The Cage*, cryptic text runs alongside each page's single panel in a dreamlike sequence unfettered from time, presenting scenes of crumbling buildings, rooms in disarray, and barren landscapes. There are no characters or speech balloons. After purchasing a copy of *The Cage* from Charlie Huisken at Toronto's legendary bookstore This Ain't the Rosedale Library, Canadian cartoonist Seth quickly saw *The Cage* as a "visionary graphic novel, far ahead of its time."[39] As he explains, "*The Cage* emerges, in some ways, from the underground comics of the late sixties and seventies. But it is so utterly unique that it is barely recognizable as part of that movement."[40] *The Cage's* uniqueness approximates it with a little-known Coach House-affiliated series, *Snore Comix*. The first issue of *Snore Comix* appeared in 1969 with a comic by Jerry of O called "Huh."[41] The group behind the series were Copithorne's avant-garde contemporaries, including Nichol and Victor Coleman, along with artists such as Greg Curnoe and members of General Idea.[42] These kinds of works, as Wershler writes, prompt us to reconsider the discursive divide between literary and comics discourses and communities. "[W]hat happens," he asks, "when a comic book crosses the fuzzy interzone that divides one community from another?"[43] Encounters with works that occupy the overlapping space of comics and Canadian literature, like *Snore Comix*, Vaughn-James's, and I'll add Copithorne's, contribute to Wershler's claim "that the barrier between the comics world and the neo-avant-gardes is more porous than it first appears."[44] I am hopeful that by placing works in dialogue in these ways, we can continue the ongoing work of expanding the field and inviting more voices into the fold, something that Copithorne's writing undoubtedly achieves.

As interest in works like those by Vaughn-James grows, considering Copithorne's graphic texts within this context allows us to expand the limited canon of early underground Canadian comics to which *Snore Comix* might also belong. Given the fact that Copithorne's work in this vein largely rejects narrative conventions and plot, I align works like *Arrangements* and *Miss Tree's Pillow Book* with what I am referring to as "graphic antinarratives." This is a term that complements scholar Hillary L. Chute's term "graphic narratives," which denotes drawn-and-written forms of storytelling, regardless of whether they fit within specific writerly genres.[45] While Chute intervenes in the discourse and offers an alternative and nuanced vocabulary for thinking through intermedia literatures such as comics and graphic novels, I offer further nuance with the term "graphic antinarrative" as a means of including drawn-and-written works that may not cohere to the norms of narrative or storytelling but follow the sequential, single-panel pattern of graphic works like Vaughn-James's. When

Copithorne and I discussed these kinds of works, she pointed out that works like *Miss Tree's Pillow Book* are "purposefully non-sequential" – a seeming paradox since it suggests that these works are intentionally created to appear without intention.[46] Comprising a substantial degree of autobiographical content, we can see Copithorne's work, following Chute's work on comics and life narrative, in a similar vein as works that productively provoke us to think about women as seeing subjects and, in turn, subjects who are seen through their artistic works. And further, we can see Copithorne's graphic antinarratives as works that "investigate concerns relegated to the silence and invisibility of the private"[47] and elements of life often overlooked as esteemed artistic subjects. The above-mentioned page from *Arrangements* is one such example. While texts like this and *Miss Tree's* may not present a coherent narrative, they materialize and give form to Copithorne's inner and outer visions as she is situated within particular times, spaces, and histories.

Reflecting on the private and autobiographical aspects of Copithorne's writing, Tallman muses that her "words have increasingly come into location on the page or in the voice in relationship to a larger context, often indicated by drawings, in which they are located alongside other objects in life, corresponding closely to clothes, or furniture, the kitchen, warmth for herself and her cat."[48] Tallman's description corresponds to my comments in the previous section regarding how her poetry acknowledges the interplay between human agency and matter's vibrance, yet he describes this as "a deliberate simplicity in order to resolve complicated inner reactions."[49] While Copithorne's poetry may in some cases register her responses and reactions to "objects in life," those responses are hardly representative of *simplicity*. On the contrary, Copithorne's writing in this vein registers the complexity of her relationship to matter and materiality, appreciating its forms and functions as agents that shape and structure lived experience. I would like to trust that Tallman's characterization is only inadvertently patronizing, but it suggests a viewpoint that sees Copithorne's writing as concerned with inconsequential domestic matters that have personal significance but little public import.

Each page in *Arrangements* is unlike the others, but a significant portion of them blends art and private life. The idea of the *arrangement* is an organizing principle for this text – arrangements of text and image, arrangements of objects, people, and places. In the tradition of an illustrator's sketchbook (which can be conceived as a visual analogue to the written diary), Copithorne documents various moments in her life: her cat, plants, a bearded man, books, cleaning products, and so on. Copithorne is also experimenting with page arrangement. There is no narrative or plot that coheres the sequence; thus I identify this work as a book of process and practice – a verbal-visual diary, with each page dedicated to a different sight, mood, feeling, or idea. "That these things," she writes above an outdoor scene in *Arrangements*, "bicycle, / plant, chair, gentle cat, symbols of inner goal / supply their own light. Omens of wind, cold / spring bite, knowledge that nothing lasts."[50] These representational scenes are seemingly reflective of the importance Copithorne places on presence and an appreciation for the objects, spaces, and people that shape her lived experience. They are also representative of a woman's private space and, by framing them on the page, she identifies these scenes as worthy of artifice. They offer us a method for visualizing Copithorne's life and present it to us with an intimacy that's similar in kind to the intimacy of her visual and concrete poetry. Their hand-drawn quality represents what Chute calls the "subjective mark of the body"[51] and frames the world as it is seen through her vision. In another untitled piece in *Arrangements*, Copithorne draws her own hand writing on a page while her cat Jasmine sleeps on her wrist.[52] The text on the page is a diary entry, with the speaker (represented by the hand) musing on love and relationships of nonattachment, which returns us to the subject of unrequited love that we occasionally find in her work. In this case, though, not only do we have a reminder that these are texts marked by a woman's body, but also a private expression of her desire that would otherwise likely be excluded from public discourse.

Miss Tree's Pillow Book is another graphic antinarrative that makes a compelling intervention into the traditions of comics and literature by further combining graphic work with life writing. Completely hand drawn and handwritten, *Miss Tree's Pillow Book* is visually similar to *Arrangements*; however, the title aligns this text with a specific para-literary tradition of the same name – the pillow book. The most famous and widely praised example of such work is *The Pillow Book of Sei Shōnagon*, composed by the Japanese poet and lady-in-waiting to Empress Sadako; Ivan Morris published an English translation of the book in 1967 with Oxford University Press. The "pillow book" has become the name of a subgenre of diaristic writing that describes "a type of informal book of notes which men and women composed when they retired to their rooms in the evening and which they kept near their sleeping place."[53] The texts that comprise a pillow book are not typically connected by plot or any strong narrative sense; rather they document daily life in a miscellany of lists, thoughts, observations, dreams, and more. According to Morris, "the arrangement" of *The Pillow Book of Sei Shōnagon* "is desultory and confusing," yet "part of its charm lies precisely in its rather bizarre, haphazard arrangement."[54] Shōnagon's private life is on display; the text conveys her observations and opinions about the weather, visitors, family life, and more. It is a private endeavour meant for the enjoyment of the author, a textual space wherein she is unfettered from external influence and censors.

Miss Tree's Pillow Book takes up this tradition and extends it to a visual mode in a graphic pseudo-diary, styled like Vaughn-James' *The Cage* with one panel per page. Some pages are dated like a traditional diary, but really what distinguishes the passage of time across the work is the stark difference between subject matter and style. Taken one way, *Miss Tree's Pillow Book* reads as though, much like a practising illustrator, Copithorne sat down to play, document daily occurrences and thoughts, and visually outline ideas. *Miss Tree's Pillow Book,* despite the occasional appearance of a character named Miss Tree (a pun on mystery), is aligned with the pillow book's conventions; it is a book of miscellany, reflections, musings, and observations. There are remarks about the weather ("Such a beautiful day! It's hard to concentrate!"), snippets of news ("C.B.C. announces another space / ship has just taken off"), philosophical queries ("What has both space & duration?"), and whimsical sexuality ("Chicken looked up at the huge falling piece of sky & / asked do you love me? The sky replied 'the myth of / the vaginal orgasm will now be received.' So then they – / as the radio says – came together"). The drawing style also varies across the text, sometimes quite sketchy but other times refined, fulsome, and self-conscious – ranging from realistic still-life drawings to icons of lightning bolts and hearts to abstract swirls and designs. In this way, *Miss Tree's Pillow Book* feels like a book of process and experimentation that is dreamlike in its composition. Copithorne's diaristic writing – like her pillow book – dissolves the boundaries between the public and private and life and art while representing resistance to conventional literature. Instead, these kinds of works are reflective of her commitment to presence and visual exploration and to herself as an artist.

Locating works like *Miss Tree's Pillow Book* or *Arrangements* within the discourse of comics may be met with resistance by some in the comics community. However, I hope that some readers will be willing to consider the implications of conceiving Copithorne's work within this purview. On *Snore Comix,* Campbell points out that most comic collectors would not recognize these as "comic books at all" and concludes that "*Snore Comix* is really only worth discussing as a series of comics because the creators decided to refer to them as such."[55] Some might make a similar argument about Copithorne's intermixture of word and image. Given that the creators of *Snore Comix* invoke comics as the genre to which these works belong, they are aligning themselves with an avant-garde tradition of art making that, in this case, sought to expand the conventions of the genre. Seth recognizes this same quality in Vaughan-James's *The Cage*, and adding Copithorne to this discourse can only expand it in productive ways, notably by prompting us to consider the Canadian avant-garde comic as a site of feminist cultural production. The work of Vaughn-James and *Snore Comix* are aligned with Copithorne's boundaryless purview; they challenge the comic's central features and, in turn, complicate the relationship between text and image and, in her work, art and life.

Revelationary Writing: Drawing from Life and Community Work

Beyond her comic-adjacent work, Copithorne extended her interest in softening the edges between art and life to other art-istic practices, perhaps most immediately visible in her work as a dancer. Copithorne danced as part of UBC professor Helen Goodwin's TheCo group, which often performed at the Sound Gallery in Vancouver's Kitsilano area. Goodwin – a co-founder of Intermedia – was a central figure in the Vancouver scene whose artistic philosophy was a "key influence on the interdisciplinary blend of Intermedia's work, much of which featured a 'live art' focus that was about situating art in the body and conceiving movement within visual art parameters,"[56] principles that directly translate into Copithorne's work as she situates the body at the centre of her writing. Gregg Simpson fondly remembers one of Copithorne's performances, loosely choreographed by Goodwin, that involved Copithorne as a dancer, music by the infamous Vancouver free jazz band the Al Neil Trio, and a film by artist Sam Perry. "One memorable solo piece," he recalls, "involved Copithorne improvising a dance which evoked flying to one of the Trio's melancholic ballads, with Perry's projected film of an actual flying bird playing over her. It was one of the best pieces in the collective repertoire."[57] Copithorne synchronized her motions with music and film and recalls that her arm movements mirrored the undulating wings of a seagull in flight, underscoring the centrality of presence in her work and how flows between music, image, and body mutually inform each other.

This folding of body and lived experience into artifice aligns Copithorne with other luminary feminist artists and writers who rejected masculinist art practices and criticism while overtly engaging with identity, gender politics, and social taboos, artists such as Carolee Schneemann and performances like her *Interior Scroll*, staged in 1975 and 1977. In this performance, a fully dressed Schneemann approaches a long, dimly lit table carrying two sheets. She undresses, wraps herself in one of the sheets and climbs onto the table. She then drops the sheet, retaining only an apron to cover herself, applies paint to her body, and begins to read from her book *Cézanne, She Was a Great Painter* while striking model-like poses. She then removes the apron, slowly draws a narrow scroll from her vagina, and reads it aloud. The scroll contains a prose poem capturing "a conversation with 'a structuralist film-maker' in which the artist sets intuition and bodily processes, traditionally associated with 'woman,' against traditionally 'male' notions of order and rationality."[58] The structuralist filmmaker uses such distinctions of "order" and "rationality" to denigrate women's art, a critique that, as noted above, Godard would repurpose and reclaim in her writing on the feminist avant-garde and the "ex-centrique." As art historian Alisia Chase explains, "the reproving comments in the poem echoed the constant criticism aimed at feminist artwork of the early '70s: that by virtue of its focus on a female creator's life and subjectivity, it wasn't, nor could ever hope to be, up to artistic snuff."[59] While Tallman's description of Copithorne's writing above does not go quite so far as the unnamed filmmaker in Schneemann's *Interior Scroll*, there is an unsettling resonance in his and the filmmaker's comments that Schneemann critiques. Chase isolates a telling part of the performance, wherein Schneemann recounts the male filmmaker stating that,

THERE ARE CERTAIN FILMS
WE CANNOT LOOK AT:
THE PERSONAL CLUTTER
THE PERSISTENCE OF FEELINGS
THE HAND-TOUCH SENSIBILITY
THE DIARISTIC IMPULSE
THE PAINTERLY MESS
THE DENSE GESTALT
THE PRIMITIVE TECHNIQUES[60]

Here, Schneeman challenges the "sexist rhetoric that dispar-
aged the 'hand-touch sensibility and primitive techniques' of
female creativity as being antithetical to the goals of modern art."[61]
Along with her own painterly messiness, diaristic impulse, and
hand-touch sensibility, Copithorne was critical of the gendered
dynamics of her literary milieu, and she folded this feminist pol-
itic into her other writing, art, and work. Rejecting prudery in
the mid-1960s, for example, she presented her body as an art-
istic subject when she worked as an undraped model for artist
Bruce Boyd's drawing classes in the Fine Arts Department at
UBC. Much like Schneemann, Copithorne takes up her body as
the means and subject for art, rejecting and responding to the
repressive paternalism and overt masculinity that dominated
her community. She offers herself to art – bare, vulnerable, and
unabashedly herself. For Copithorne and other feminist artists,
it is precisely "the personal clutter" of their lives that they want
observed to begin unsettling gendered hierarchies in art and life.

The "personal clutter" that Schneemann identifies is the quo-
tidian material and social stuff of life with which she interacts
and, in turn, across which subjectivity unfolds. The 1960s and
1970s began to see women's subjectivity and quotidian subject
matter gradually gravitate towards the centre of cultural discourse.
1966, for example, saw the groundbreaking publication of *The
Diary of Anaïs Nin*, an expurgated version of Nin's actual, personal
diaries covering her friendship with writer Henry Miller, her

psychoanalysis sessions with Otto Rank – one of Sigmund Freud's disciples – and her encounters with French avant-garde playwright Antonin Artaud. Noting its literary prowess, Miller praised Nin's diaristic writing as "a monumental confession which when given to the world will take its place beside the revelations of St. Augustine, Petronius, Abélard, Rousseau, Proust, and others."[62] Nin's diaries were among the publications of the time that shattered assumptions about women's private lives as unworthy of literary status. That Nin bore consequence for Copithorne is evident in the drawing of Nin's diary partially visible in a poem-drawing in *Arrangements,* resting beneath a book of Blake's poetry.[63] The appearance of Nin's diary in a piece that depicts Copithorne's own "personal clutter" suggests the centrality of life writing to her work. Scholars Carole Gerson and Yvan Lamonde see this particular poem-drawing as a notable work in her oeuvre and central to movements in the 1960s and 1970s, wherein "artists envisioned new relationships among books, images, and words, questioning traditional generic distinctions by turning paintings, drawings, and even quilts into texts to be read,"[64] and I would add questioning the distinction between art and life. Widely recognized as a masterful diarist, Nin describes her diary thus: "The Diary dealing always with the immediate present, the warm, the near, being written at white heat, developed a love of the living moment, of the immediate emotional reaction to experience, which revealed the power of recreation to lie in the sensibilities rather than in memory or critical intellectual perception."[65] Nin's description of the diary as a form of embracing the "immediate," the "warm," and the "near" echoes Tallman's descriptions of Copithorne's autobiographical writing. While Tallman seems to diminish this kind of writing, it is exactly this type of writing – representative of her worldly experience – that Nin claims should be a central literary subject in the mid-twentieth century. For Nin, the relationship between the interiority and exteriority of human experience must be a principal theme, since that is where we can see the true self revealed. From writing her diaries, Nin claims she learned "that it is in moments of emotional crisis that human beings reveal themselves most accurately. I learned to choose heightened moments because they are moments of revelation."[66] And while Nin privileges moments of crisis and transformation when documenting her personal and artistic life, Copithorne concerns herself with the revelations that greet her every day, regardless of how mundane they may seem, and those that are sometimes unseen.

The importance Copithorne places on small transformative moments is articulated in one of her few prose works, *Heart's Tide* (1972), where she writes, "Revelation may be essentially quiet and not in the least dramatic, especially to one brought up in our insidiously tense and violent culture,"[67] a seeming counterpoint to Nin's privileging of crisis. In our private discussions of this work, Copithorne informed me that it is loosely based on real events, though she did not reveal what is fiction and what is fact in the text. I will note that the narrator mirrors Copithorne in some recognizable ways – her geographical location in Vancouver and the West Coast area; her interest in meditation and Buddhism; her frequent trips to the United States at that time. Some character names also have conspicuous similarities to real people, including the twice-mentioned Maxine, who could perhaps be Vancouver poet Maxine Gadd. None of this is certain. Certainty regarding the facts, however, is of less importance; rather it is the realism of the diary form that stands out, since it so starkly contrasts the aesthetic extremes of her intermedia writing. While that vector of her work is very much "outside the bounds," *Heart's Tide* reads like an actual diary. It follows the diary's conventions with dated entries and, much like a personal diary, it follows unconventional story shapes. *Heart's Tide* – in a way that is similar to *Miss Tree's Pillow Book* – catalogues day-to-day thoughts, encounters, and events as they arise. These textual elements add a degree of realism to its form, since we have a narrator who is enjoying the freedom diaristic writing offers. The notebook – like the journal and diary – is a "place to play, a safe haven away from our embedded editor,"[68] and *Heart's Tide* embraces exactly that kind of freedom in its approach to storytelling.

Mixing genre and style, *Heart's Tide* comprises a series of diary entries that are punctuated by four short stories, three of which are definitely about a character named Hanna – as a child, a teenager, and a young woman; the fourth features a nameless young woman, likely Hanna, and a mysterious man named Bartolome. Written in constrained prosaic bursts and a stream-of-consciousness style, the diary entries around these stories track the day-to-day of the nameless narrator while exploring the social and political dynamics of gender. Copithorne goes to great lengths to cultivate a semi-fictional representation of what would otherwise be a woman's "personal clutter" and declares it to be of public import. While there are manifold threads woven into the text, sexuality and the complexities of heteronormative relationships dominate the narrator's consciousness. Without necessarily moralizing on these issues, *Heart's Tide* seemingly interrogates the project of the sexual liberation movement of the 1960s and early 1970s – coinciding with the second-wave feminist and women's liberation movements – and its claim to challenge codes of behaviour related to heterosexuality and monogamy, its pathway to the normalization of premarital sex, and its push towards wider abortion access. Though the narrator is sometimes empowered by her sexuality and desirous pursuits, she is also wary of the men that come and go in her life. This includes one man named Greg, with whom she shares an extramarital affair. She desires him but knows, given his unwillingness to leave his family, that their relationship is physical and transient. In one instance, her desire for the unavailable Greg prompts her to question her own well-being. "Greg came by. He seems kind. I must be mad, he has a wife and son,"[69] and then later, after sex, she feels rather demoralized: "Yesterday Greg came and we made love. He hasn't called today. The void. Always ending up looking at yourself." The narrator's pleasurable but confusing relationship with Greg leads her to spend much of her time musing on love, relationships, and gender roles.

The first of *Heart's Tide* Hanna stories is "Sea Change," featuring a five-year-old Hanna who, knowing that "she should not think of travelling so far from home," is enamoured by the "ocean beauty," and sets off by herself anyway. The second, "The Trail Through," narrates sixteen-year-old Hanna's encounter with an unknown man at a gallery in Vancouver. Hanna, on her "first female adventure," is exploring her powers of attraction and has caught the attention of a man who invites her to join him for coffee. As their encounter continues, Hanna becomes increasingly agitated – "She felt a rising inside her, her hands slipped on her cup" – and, overwhelmed, she anxiously excuses herself to return home to her grandmother. In the third of these stories, "Early One Morning," Hanna is now staying at the Stella Hotel, a "run down, crummy, hideaway for gentle people crushed by the city machine." Perhaps the most climactic story of the collection (discussed in more detail below), this episode vividly portrays a difficult stillbirth for Hanna who, at the Stella Hotel's Christmas dinner, discovers that she is unexpectedly pregnant. The final story of this sequence, "Bartolome," who is mentioned in the opening diary entry of *Heart's Tide* – "Told Elli the story about Bartolome last night" – revealing that the writer of these stories is also the narrator of the diary, which suggests that Hanna may be a fictional representation of the diary writer (whether that writer is Copithorne, however, remains unclear). In "Bartolome," the nameless character meets the mysterious Bartolome on a bus in Seattle and, attracted to him, opts to miss her connecting bus in Portland to San Francisco to spend the night with him in a hotel, a decision she will ultimately regret. If we assume Hanna is the character in the final story, the sequence captures Hanna in a series of stories, depicting her transition from innocence to experience. Hanna's experiences, beginning with her encounter with the open world as a five-year-old girl and becoming more entwined with the complexity of gender and sexuality, outline various forms of struggle and challenge that a young woman would face at the time.

Gender and sexuality, as presented in *Heart's Tide*, are connected to the broader shifting dynamics at the time, and their manifestation in social and political discourse in Vancouver and

Canada more broadly. "Our premier," says the diary's narrator, "who rules this province as a heavy dictator talking about the Nations of the Pacific Rim and the Prime Minister says he will put forward a bill which could remove the illegality of abortion in one day. Women's Liberation stand on street corners asking for this every weekend." *Heart's Tide* was published one year after the active period – from 1968 to 1971 – of the Vancouver Women's Caucus, a feminist organization that led, among other things, campaigns to decriminalize abortion. This is likely the group the narrator of *Heart's Tide* is referring to "on street corners." One of the Caucus's most notable campaigns was the initiation of the 1970 cross-Canada protest, known as the Abortion Caravan, to oppose the 1969 amendments to the Criminal Code, which only incrementally amended the status of abortion from widespread criminalization to legalization under specific circumstances. Unsatisfied with this meagre development, the Abortion Caravan – starting in Vancouver and ending in Ottawa – sought to have abortion removed from the Criminal Code altogether.

In *Heart's Tide*, the narrator's treatment of abortion is not exactly activist-oriented – there are seemingly no calls to action – but she is acutely aware of the shifts underway, and we follow her as she grapples with what the sexual liberation and women's liberation movements might mean to her. One of the most climactic and illustrative moments in *Heart's Tide* is an extended section where Hanna, unexpectedly pregnant, goes to the hospital seeking assistance. Leading up to the visit, Hanna is distressed, suffering from painful abdominal cramps, and is waiting for a friend to take her there. The eventual visit to the emergency room echoes a similar scene in the August 1934 section of *The Diary of Anaïs Nin*, where Nin documents her own miscarriage after a failed abortion: "It does not belong in my life," writes Nin, "for I have too many people to take care of. I have, already, too many children."[70] Like Nin, Hanna is disparaged by hospital staff, who interrogate her about the absence of the father and falsely accuse her: "Where did you have the abortion?" they ask, and this "assumption horrified her because it wasn't true." Just as in Nin, the fetus is eventually passed. "Suddenly she was gone," says the narrator in *Heart's Tide*, and "a consciousness emerged beyond it all," a consciousness that likely left the narrator forever changed. This immensely difficult scene in *Heart's Tide* demonstrates Copithorne's sensitivity to issues like abortion and the harrowing conditions many women faced, while also recognizing the significant impacts of lost pregnancies. The "she" that disappears in the quotation above is likely not the fetus, but a part of Hanna that transformed during the experience.

Hanna's experience highlights the stigma that abortion carried in Vancouver and Canada at the time and underscores the monumental challenges women face to have control over their bodies and reproductive rights. On the other hand, it also highlights one of the complexities of the sexual liberation movement. While the movement is sometimes said to have contributed to the normalization of premarital sex – something the diary's narrator enjoys – Hanna's experience with the Vancouver hospital reveals how this movement also, to some degree, privileged men who may not have had to endure the outcomes of transient sexual relationships. Women who become pregnant, like Hanna, are forced to face the alienating conditions of a health-care system that devalues the real-life conditions of women. In these ways, *Heart's Tide* reveals the complexity of shifting gender dynamics at the time, and Copithorne, as the author, carefully explores the challenges that these social and cultural changes posed. In the ways discussed above, *Heart's Tide* takes the so-called "personal clutter" of women's lives (both Hanna's and the diary's narrator's), announces their public import, and in its own way brings it into dialogue with larger questions about Canadian social politics at the time. In subtle and not-so-subtle ways, the texts in *Heart's Tide* are revealing stories that are "essentially quiet and not in the least dramatic." They are stories that reveal the silent discomfort felt by Hanna and the narrator, indicative of the experiences of many women that would otherwise be ignored in a male-dominated culture.

The kinds of sociopolitical engagements readers will see represented in works like *Heart's Tide* are representative of what Gregg Simpson calls Copithorne's efforts to break "the grip of the paternalistic elites."[71] These texts provide opportunities for discussions of subjectivity, body, and experience, using art as a means of intervention into social contexts – another way Copithorne sought to blur art and life. As noted in "A Personal and Informal Introduction and Checklist Regarding Some Larger Poetry Enterprises in Vancouver and Primarily in the Earlier Part of the 1960s," collected here, Copithorne understood art and politics as closely aligned. In fact, her sociopolitical engagement spilled into life itself. "One thing that tied my experiences together," she writes, "was the political aspect of my life. I had very little time or energy, but I did manage to go to a variety of political events and marches … these included the antiwar and peace movements, socialist activities, and feminism."[72] To this end, Copithorne was also a force in and of herself, serving and contributing to Vancouver's creative communities with her magazine of writing and image, *Returning*, published from July 1972 until May 1973.[73] This was an endeavour that Copithorne ended only because, as she explained to me, she was getting such a positive response that she could not maintain work on the series. With poetry, prose, photography, and drawings adorning its pages, *Returning* features many then up-and-coming stars of Canadian literature, including Daphne Marlatt, bill bissett, George Bowering, and bpNichol, alongside less well-known but equally important figures such as Mona Fertig, Maxine Gadd, Beth Jankola, and more.[74] Though this was a short-lived publication venture for Copithorne, it reveals her position within a transnational literary and artistic network stretching beyond Vancouver's city lines and illustrates for us her commitment to the cultivation of literary community.

In its variance and brilliance, *Another Order* is prismatic, capturing decades of Copithorne's inimitable traversal of genre, form, language, media, and mode that defy any attempt to narrowly define her practice. If we were to enumerate the many intersecting identities that comprise her work, we can say that, among many things, Judith Copithorne is an intermedia worker, poet, story-teller, diarist, comics artist, visual artist, community organizer, feminist, antiwar activist, socialist, peace advocate, editor, publisher, dancer, and model, and an inspiration to many generations of writers that follow in her wake. Across each page, audiences can see evidence of her revelatory work that opened the field of intermedial avant-garde writing in Canada, which has been dominated by masculine personalities for far too long. With the publications selected for *Another Order*, we see Copithorne's lifelong commitment to art that brings writing into dialogue with practices of feminist embodiment, autobiography, and more. Needless to say, my selection in *Another Order* is not exhaustive, and I hope that it will only light a desire in the reader to seek more of Copithorne's writing and to articulate the multifaceted ways that her work fits within broader artistic lineages and traditions. Copithorne's writing and art making spring not only as a lively and spirited force of imagination but as a powerful vision, a vision of another order, another way of being in and engaging the world aesthetically, socially, and politically, to which we can all aspire.

Endnotes

1 Lorna Brown, "GLUT: Beginning with Language," in *Beginning with the Seventies*, ed. Lorna Brown, Greg Gibson, and Jana Tyner (Vancouver: Morris and Helen Belkin Art Gallery, 2020), 44.

2 See *Surprising Writing* in this collection.

3 Dick Higgins with Hannah Higgins, "Intermedia," *Leonardo* 34, no. 1 (February 2001): 49, muse.jhu.edu/pub/6/article/19618.

4 Carole Itter, "Carole Itter with Lorna Brown," interview by Lorna Brown, *Ruins in Process: Vancouver Art in the Sixties*, ed. Lorna Brown, Morris and Helen Belkin Art Gallery and Grunt Gallery, June 1, 2009, vancouverartinthesixties.com/interviews/carol-itter.

5 Gregg Simpson, email message to author, July 26, 2022.

6 Lori Emerson, "women dirty concrete poets," *loriemerson – dot net* (blog), May 4, 2011, loriemerson.net/2011/05/04/women-dirty-concrete-poets/.

7 Amanda Earl, "Amanda Earl," in *Judith: Women Making Visual Poetry* (Malmö, Sweden: Timglaset Editions, 2021), 60.

8 Judith Copithorne, "This was drawn last year …," *blewointment* 2, no. 4 (September 1964): unpaginated.

9 Gregory Betts, *Finding Nothing: The VanGardes, 1959–1975* (Toronto: University of Toronto Press, 2021), 192.

10 Caroline Bayard, *The New Poetics in Canada and Quebec: From Concretism to Post-Modernism* (Toronto: University of Toronto Press, 1989), 141.

11 See "Squaring the Vowels" in this collection.

12 bpNichol, ed., *The Cosmic Chef: An Evening of Concrete* (Ottawa: Oberon Press, 1970), unpaginated. Available online on "the official bpNichol archive": www.bpnichol.ca/sites/default/files/archives/document/The%20Cosmic%20Chef.pdf.

13 See the final page of *Arrangements* in this collection.

14 Peter Schwenger, *Asemic: The Art of Writing* (Minneapolis: University of Minnesota Press, 2019), 1.

15 Tim Gaze, *asemic movement* 1 (January 2008), issuu.com/eexxiitt/docs/asemic movement1.

16 Henri Michaux, translated by Schwenger and quoted on page 24 of his book.

17 Schwenger, *Asemic*, 1.

18 Some readers may be interested in my article "'my body of bliss': Judith

Copithorne's Concrete Poetry in the 1960s and 1970s" (*Canadian Poetry* 83 [Fall–Winter 2018]: 14–39, canadianpoetry.org/wp-content/uploads/2020/03/Studies-1-83.pdf), where I first explored the feminist work of Copithorne's writing. I revisit some of those points again in the remainder of this section.

19 Barbara Godard, "Ex-centriques, Eccentric, Avant-Garde: Women and Modernism in the Literatures of Canada," *Room of One's Own* 8, no. 4 (Winter 1984): 64, doi.org/10.25071/1923-9408.23492.

20 Bayard, *The New Poetics in Canada and Quebec*, 164.

21 Sianne Ngai, "Raw Matter: A Poetics of Disgust," *Open Letter* 10, no. 1 (1998): 116, publish.uwo.ca/%7Efdavey/c/10.1.htm.

22 See Beaulieu's "an afterword after words: notes toward a concrete poetic" in *fractal economies* (Vancouver: Talonbooks, 2006).

23 Barrie Tullett, *Typewriter Art: A Modern Anthology* (London: Laurence King Publishing, 2014), 52.

24 Ngai, "Raw Matter," 116.

25 Steve McCaffery, "Bill Bissett: A Writing Outside Writing," in *North of Intention: Critical Writings, 1973–1986* (New York: Roof Books; Toronto, Nightwood Editions, 2000), 93.

26 Darren Wershler [credited as Darren Wershler-Henry], *The Iron Whim: A Fragmented History of Typewriting* (Ithaca: Cornell University Press, 2007), 91.

27 See *Heart's Tide* in this collection for this and subsequent quotes in this paragraph.

28 Brown, "GLUT," 44.

29 See *Horizon* in this collection.

30 Anyone who would like to see a fuller range of Copithorne's digital work should look towards her Flickr account pages (flic.kr/ps/2ZjJ3y), where she uploaded work from 2007 to 2014 and 2015 to 2017, respectively.

31 *Oxford English Dictionary*, s.v. "digital, *n.* and *adj.*," July 2023, doi.org/10.1093/OED/1297556308.

32 Judith Copithorne, *Phases / Phrases* (British Columbia: Trainwreck Press, 2019).

33 See *Brackets & Boundaries {concrete & other accretions}* in this collection.

34 See ibid.

35 Scott McCloud, *Understanding Comics: The Invisible Art* (New York: Harper Perennial, 1994), 9.

36 See *Arrangements* in this collection.

37 See *Miss Tree's Pillow Book* in this collection.

38 Robert C. Harvey, "Comedy at the Juncture of Word and Image: The Emergence of the Modern Magazine Gag Cartoon Reveals the Vital Blend," in *The Language of Comics: Word and Image*, ed. Robin Varnum and Christina T. Gibbons (Jackson: University Press of Mississippi, 2001), 75–76.

39 Seth, "Man Fears Time, but Time Fears Only Pyramids," introduction to Martin

Vaughn-James, *The Cage* (Toronto: Coach House Press, 2013), 6.

40 Seth, "Man Fears Time," 6.

41 brian Campbell, "Snore Comix," *Comic Book Daily (blog)*, October 12, 2020, www.comicbookdaily.com/columns/forgotten-silver/snore-comix/.

42 While little has been written on these rare publications, brian Campbell's research determined that central figures behind the (maybe) seven planned issues of the series included Nichol, members of General Idea (AA Bronson, Jorge Zontal, and Felix Partz), Coleman, and Curnoe. Regarding *Snore Comix*'s publication history, Campbell writes, "there were nine issues of the series, 'but not really.' His contact [explained] to him that, 'There were seven but then again (being Coach House) there weren't. The first two were edited by Jerry ofO (the second with input from Victor Coleman and bpNichol). The third was edited by Victor [Coleman] with help from Michael Tims (aka AA Bronson) who's credited alone with editing it in the catalogue.' The contact then explained that issues number four and five were General Idea conceptions and that [Vincent] Trasov was part of their inner circle at the time. Issue number six was a spontaneous creation by Gerry Gilbert for Victor Coleman's poetry class, while issue number seven was 'all Jim Lang.' A subsequent issue number seven was also created, with either Coleman or AA Bronson editing it. A final issue was created and distributed in 1994 under the name 'IRATA' to commemorate the induction of bpNichol Lane in Toronto" (see brian Campbell's "The Coach House Nose Who's Who," *Comic Book Daily* [blog], November 9, 2020, www.comicbookdaily.com/columns/forgotten-silver/the-coach-house-nose-whos-who/).

43 Darren Wershler, "Canadian Comics Studies, Canons, the Coach House, and *The Cage*," *Canadian Literature / Littérature canadienne* 249 (November 14, 2022), ojs.library.ubc.ca/index.php/canlit/article/view/196869.

44 Ibid.

45 The *novel* aspect of "graphic novel," for example, is suggestive only of work that is also a fictitious narrative following the writerly conventions of conflict, plot, and character.

46 Judith Copithorne, phone call with author, August 4, 2022.

47 Hillary L. Chute, *Graphic Women: Life Narrative and Contemporary Comics*, Gender and Culture Series (New York: Columbia University Press, 2010), 4.

48 Warren Tallman, "Wonder Merchants: Modernist Poetry in Vancouver during the 1960's," *Boundary 2*, vol. 3, no. 1 (Autumn 1974): 86, doi.org/10.2307/302408.

49 Tallman, "Wonder Merchants," 86.

50 See *Arrangements* in this collection.

51 Chute, *Graphic Women*, 11.

52 See *Arrangements* in this collection.

53 Ivan Morris, introduction to his translation of *The Pillow Book of Sei Shōnagon* (New York: Penguin Books, [1967] 1987), 11.

54 Morris, introduction to *The Pillow Book*, 13.

55 Campbell, "The Coach House Nose Who's Who."

56 Kaija Pepper, "Helen Goodwin and Intermedia: Toward Live Art in Vancouver," in *Beginning with the Seventies*, ed. Lorna Brown, Greg Gibson, and Jana Tyner (Vancouver: Morris and Helen Belkin Art Gallery, 2020), 157.

57 Gregg Simpson, "*The Sound Gallery*: The Official History of the Sound Gallery, Motion Studio, the Trips Festival, and the Founding of Intermedia," *The Art of Gregg Simpson*, 2018, greggsimpson.com/soundgallerymotionstudio.htm.

58 Elizabeth Manchester, "Carolee Schneemann: *Interior Scroll* (1975)," Tate, 2003, tate.org.uk/art/artworks/schneemann-interior-scroll-p13282.

59 Alisia Chase, "You Must Look at the Personal Clutter: Diaristic Indulgence, Female Adolescence, and Feminist Autobiography," in *Drawing from Life: Memory and Subjectivity in Comic Art*, ed. Jane Tolmie (Jackson: University Press of Mississippi, 2013), 208.

60 Carolee Schneemann, "Reading from *The Interior Scroll*" (1973–1976), Tate, 2003, tate.org.uk/art/artworks/schneemann-interior-scroll-p13282.

61 Chase, "You Must Look at the Personal Clutter," 208.

62 Henry Miller, "Un Etre Etoilique" (1937), in *The Henry Miller Reader*, ed. Lawrence Durrell (New York: New Directions Books, 1959), 287.

63 See *Arrangements* in this collection.

64 Carole Gerson and Yvan Lamonde, "Books and Reading in Canadian Art," in *History of the Book in Canada, vol. 3, 1918–1980*, ed. Carole Gerson and Jacques Michon (Toronto: University of Toronto Press, 2007), 79.

65 Anaïs Nin, "On Writing," in *On Writing*, ed. William Burford, "Outcast" Chapbooks series (Yonkers, NY: Alicat Bookshop, 1947), 21.

66 Nin, "On Writing," 22.

67 See *Heart's Tide* in this collection.

68 Jennifer New, introduction to *Drawing from Life: The Journal as Art* (New York: Princeton Architectural Press, 2005), 13.

69 See *Heart's Tide* in this collection for this and further quotes in this section.

70 Anaïs Nin, *The Diary of Anaïs Nin*, vol. 5, 1947–1955, ed. Gunther Stuhlman (New York: Swallow Press and Harcourt, Brace & World, 1966), 338.

71 Gregg Simpson, email message to author, July 26, 2022.

72 See "A Personal and Informal Introduction and Checklist Regarding Some Larger Poetry Enterprises in Vancouver and Primarily in the Earlier Part of the 1960s" in this collection.

73 To be precise, the first two issues are titled *Returning*, while the third issue is titled *Return*. The first two issues were supported by a Vancouver Local Initiatives grant. Issue one appeared in July 1972; issue two appeared in August 1972; issue three appeared in May 1973.

74 *Returning Press One* (1972) features "David Leicester, Claire Stannard, Bill Hoffer, Fred Douglas, cd connor, Beth Jankola, Bonnie Varney, Mona Fertig, Les Hamer, Carole Fisher, Shana Fox, Robert Corse, Judith Copithorne, and Michael Chiasson"; *Returning Two* (1972) features "Fred Douglas, Robert Corse, bill bissett, c.d. connor, George Bowering, Bill Hoffer, Claire Stannard, Judith Copithorne, Michael Melanson, Beth Jankola, bp Nichol, Jone Pane, Mona Fertig, Victor Coleman, Peter Stevens, Stan Persky, Judith Williams Fraser, Maxine Gadd, and Daphne Marlatt"; *Return : Three* (1973) features "Audrey Doray, Carole Itter, James Reaney, Maxine Gadd, David UU, and Gladys Hindmarch.

Works Cited

Bayard, Caroline. *The New Poetics in Canada and Quebec: From Concretism to Post-Modernism.* Toronto: University of Toronto Press, 1989.

Betts, Gregory. *Finding Nothing: The VanGardes, 1959–1975.* Toronto: University of Toronto Press, 2021.

Brown, Lorna. "GLUT: Beginning with Language." In *Beginning with the Seventies*, edited by Lorna Brown, Greg Gibson, and Jana Tyner, 33–53. Vancouver: Morris and Helen Belkin Art Gallery and Information Office, 2020.

Campbell, brian. "The Coach House Nose Who's Who." *Comic Book Daily* (blog), November 9, 2020. www.comicbookdaily.com/columns/forgotten-silver/the-coach-house-nose-whos-who/.

———. "Snore Comix." *Comic Book Daily* (blog), October 12, 2020. www.comicbookdaily.com/columns/forgotten-silver/snore-comix/.

Chase, Alisia. "You Must Look at the Personal Clutter: Diaristic Indulgence, Female Adolescence, and Feminist Autobiography." In *Drawing from Life: Memory and Subjectivity in Comic Art*, edited by Jane Tolmie, 207–240. Jackson: University Press of Mississippi, 2013. doi.org/10.14325/mississippi/9781617039058.003.0010.

Chute, Hillary L. *Graphic Women: Life Narrative and Contemporary Comics.* Gender and Culture Series. New York: Columbia University Press, 2010.

Copithorne, Judith. "This was drawn last year …" *blewointment* 2, no. 4 (September 1964): unpaginated.

curry, jw. "proof no burden: a start at a Judith Copithorne checklist." *1cent* 400 / *news notes* 13 (March 15, 2009): unpaginated.

Earl, Amanda, ed. *Judith: Women Making Visual Poetry.* Malmö, Sweden: Timglaset Editions, 2021.

Emerson, Lori. "women dirty concrete poets." *loriemerson – dot net* (blog), May 4, 2011. loriemerson.net/2011/05/04/women-dirty-concrete-poets/.

Gaze, Tim. *asemic movement* 1 (January 2008): 1–13. issuu.com/eexxiitt/docs/asemicmovement1.

Gerson, Carole, and Yvan Lamonde. "Books and Reading in Canadian Art." In *History of the Book in Canada*. Vol. 3, *1918–1980*, edited by Carole Gerson and Jacques Michon, 75–80. Toronto: University of Toronto Press, 2007.

Godard, Barbara. "Ex-centriques, Eccentric, Avant-Garde: Women and Modernism in the Literatures of Canada." *Room of One's Own* 8, no. 4 (Winter 1984): 57–75. doi.org/10.25071/1923-9408.23492.

Harvey, Robert C. "Comedy at the Juncture of Word and Image: The Emergence of the Modern Magazine Gag Cartoon Reveals the Vital Blend." In *The Language of Comics: Word and Image*, edited by Robin Varnum and Christina T. Gibbons, 75–96. Popular Culture series. Jackson: University Press of Mississippi, 2001.

Higgins, Dick, with Hannah Higgins. "Intermedia." *Leonardo* 34, no. 1 (February 2001): 49–54. muse.jhu.edu/pub/6/article/19618.

Itter, Carole. "Carole Itter with Lorna Brown." Interview by Lorna Brown. Ruins in Process: Vancouver Art in the Sixties (website). June 1, 2009. vancouverartinthesixties.com/interviews/carol-itter.

Manchester, Elizabeth. "Carolee Schneeman: *Interior Scroll* (1975)." Tate (website). November 2003. www.tate.org.uk/art/artworks/schneemann-interior-scroll-p13282.

McCaffery, Steve. "Bill Bissett: A Writing Outside Writing." In *North of Intention: Critical Writings, 1973–1986*, 93–106. New York: Roof Books; Toronto: Nightwood Editions, 2000.

McCloud, Scott. *Understanding Comics: The Invisible Art*. New York: Harper Perennial, 1994.

Michaux, Henri. *Mouvements: Soixante-quatre dessins, un poème, une postface*. Paris: Gallimard, [1951] 1982.

Miller, Henry. "Un Être Étoilique." In *The Henry Miller Reader*, edited by Lawrence Durrell. New York: New Directions Books, 1959, 287–306.

Morris, Ivan. Introduction to *The Pillowbook of Sei Shōnagon*. Translated by Ivan Morris. New York: Penguin Books, [1967] 1987.

New, Jennifer. *Drawing from Life: The Journal as Art*. New York: Princeton Architectural Press, 2005.

Ngai, Sianne. "Raw Matter: A Poetics of Disgust." *Open Letter* 10, no. 1 (Winter 1998): 98–122. publish.uwo.ca/~fdavey/c/10.1.htm.

Nichol, bp, ed. *The Cosmic Chef: An Evening of Concrete* [alternative title: *The Cosmic Chef, Glee and Perloo Memorial Society, under the Direction of Captain Poetry Presents: An Evening of Concrete, Courtesy … Oberon Cement Works*]. Ottawa: Oberon Press, 1970. www.bpnichol.ca/sites/default/files/archives/document/The%20Cosmic%20Chef.pdf.

Nin, Anaïs. *On Writing*. Edited by William Burford. "Outcast" Chapbooks series. Yonkers, NY: Alicat Bookshop, 1947.

———. *The Diary of Anaïs Nin*. Edited by Gunther Stuhlman. New York: The Swallow Press and Harcourt, Brace and World Inc., 1966.

Pepper, Kaija. "Helen Goodwin and Intermedia: Toward Live Art in Vancouver." In *Beginning with the Seventies*, edited by Lorna Brown, Greg Gibson, and Jana Tyner, 157–161. Vancouver: Morris and Helen Belkin Art Gallery and Information Office, 2020.

Sackner, Ruth, and Marvin Sackner. *The Art of Typewriting*. London: Thames and Hudson, 2015.

Schneemann, Carolee. "Reading from *The Interior Scroll*" (1973–1976). Tate (website). 2023. www.tate.org.uk/art/artworks/schneemann-interior-scroll-p13282.

Schwenger, Peter. *Asemic: The Art of Writing*. Minneapolis: University of Minnesota Press, 2019.

Shōnagon, Sei. *The Pillowbook of Sei Shōnagon*. Translated by Ivan Morris. New York: Penguin Books, [1967] 1987.

Simpson, Gregg. "The Sound Gallery: The Official History of the Sound Gallery, Motion Studio, the Trips Festival and the Founding of Intermedia." *The Art of Gregg Simpson* (website), 2018. www.greggsimpson.com/soundgallery motionstudio.htm.

Tallman, Warren. "Wonder Merchants: Modernist Poetry in Vancouver during the 1960's." *Boundary 2*, vol. 3, no. 1 (Autumn 1974): 57–90. doi.org/10.2307/302408.

Tullet, Barrie, ed. *Typewriter Art: A Modern Anthology*. London: Laurence King Publishing, 2014.

Vaughn-James, Martin. *The Cage*. Toronto: Coach House Press, 2013.

Wershler, Darren. "Canadian Comics Studies, Canons, the Coach House, and *The Cage*." *Canadian Literature / Littérature canadienne* 249 (November 14, 2022): 66–79. ojs.library.ubc.ca/index.php/canlit/article/view/196869.

Wershler, Darren [credited as Darren Wershler-Henry]. *The Iron Whim: A Fragmented History of Typewriting*. Ithaca: Cornell University Press, 2007.

VISUAL POETRY
AND
HYBRID WORKS

Meandering

1967

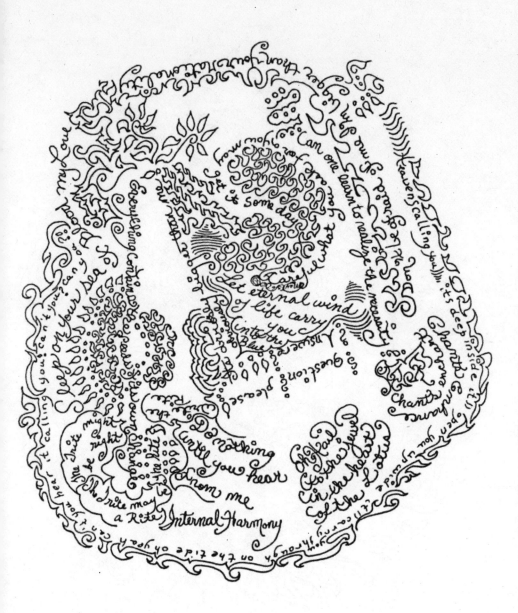

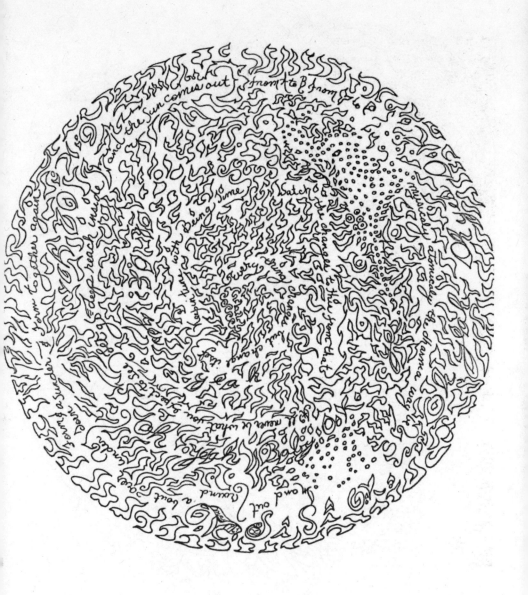

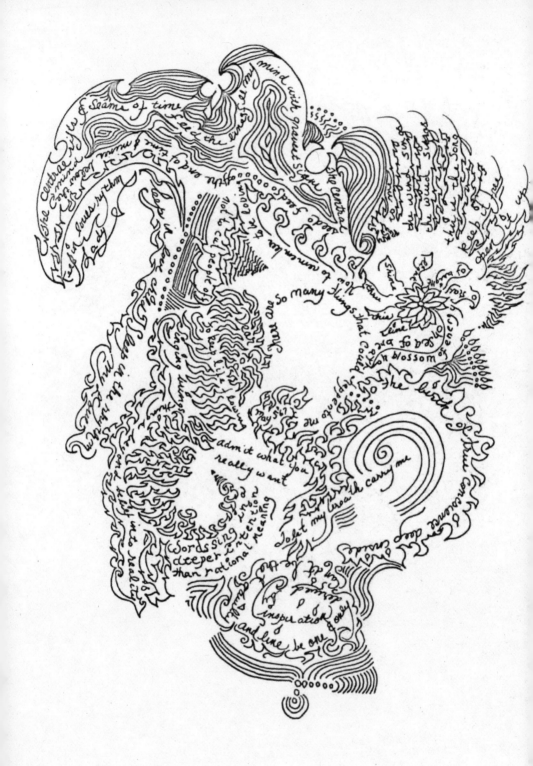

Another Order

Where Have I Been

1967

where have I been
Inside my shell
my shell is made of golden light
The song it sings so ripe and bright
Whistling like the wind at night

where have I been
far away
Inside my
of changing energy

where have I been
far removed
With it sank deep into me
and vanished into placidity

where am I
where I've always been
Slipped from illusion
into energy
Slipped from shadow
into light
Slipped from myself
into unity

Watching
Yellow bird
We heard you watching the yellow
Bird and you said
She is seeing some colours
Singing

Without resentment
without fear
let the summer
flesh
in cut
when heat of head
melts hip
heat
worlds convulsed
rhythm
unfolds

undulating
warmth from
organ to organ

released
sea breezes
blew
through garden
door
clearing
living
breathing

we need
never
destroy

The trumpet voluntary
calling me
the song of the Serpent
in sinuous violins

The Serpent moves
across the face of the deep
His seed is in me
it is born in sleep
His way to keep
until great Sun flowers
Burst into full bloom
beyond my head
Joining Sun and moon

Each part of the room glows
filled full of its own light

The refrain of love
fulfils the night

The room reflects
love's light

The Serpent
seeks across the night
he sleeps in the deep
Son of the light

The serpent
breathing fire
and pulsing life
married the moon

The serpent moves
across the face of the deeps
planting love's fire
as she, silent moon, sleeps

all dark is the mark of secret fears and sorrows which make our years ... our own frequency ... life and ... light ...

Guadalupe
moon mother
holding me
fuchsia ribbons
of vision
braided in
our hair

Everything is only process
Sitting breath indrawn
given out again
deep reach inside
and Sun comes sad again
deep reach inside
until shadows and sunlight
encompass me
guts growl and sensation
overwhelms
let go deep reach inside
see the process
engulfing me
we always meditate on
mod
on nothing anyway

Fresh green shoots of grass
the wash being hung out
on a creaking line
the changes from this to
that tingle me
nothing is everything
process

Everything is only process
let the consciousness
infuse everything

Reach this place where you
no longer progress
Only move in the flux of
seasons and tides and lunar phases
where your pressure will vary
with rain and sun
Your years return
and grow round our earth

Rain

1969

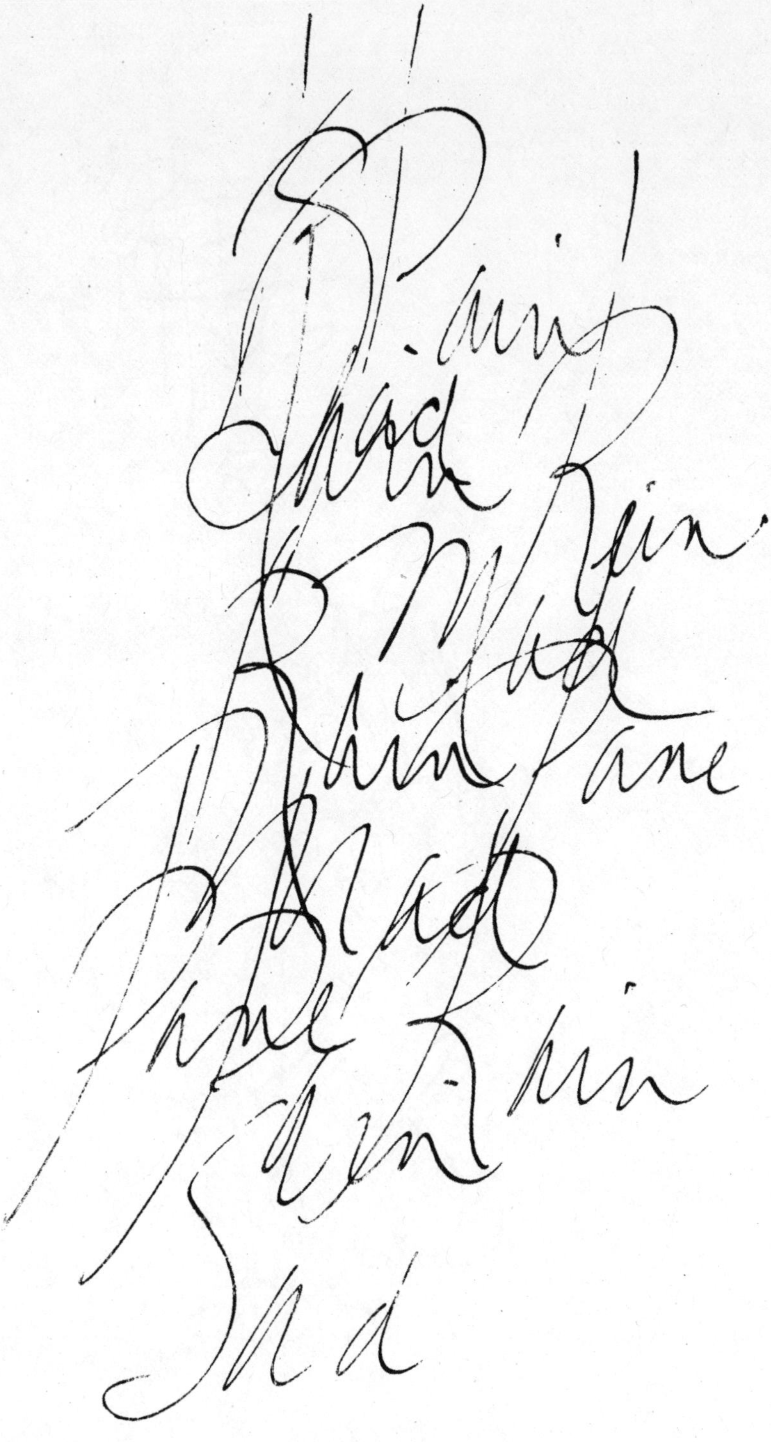

18

Another Order

Can I say
You were so long
When you
stopped loving
me?

Another Order

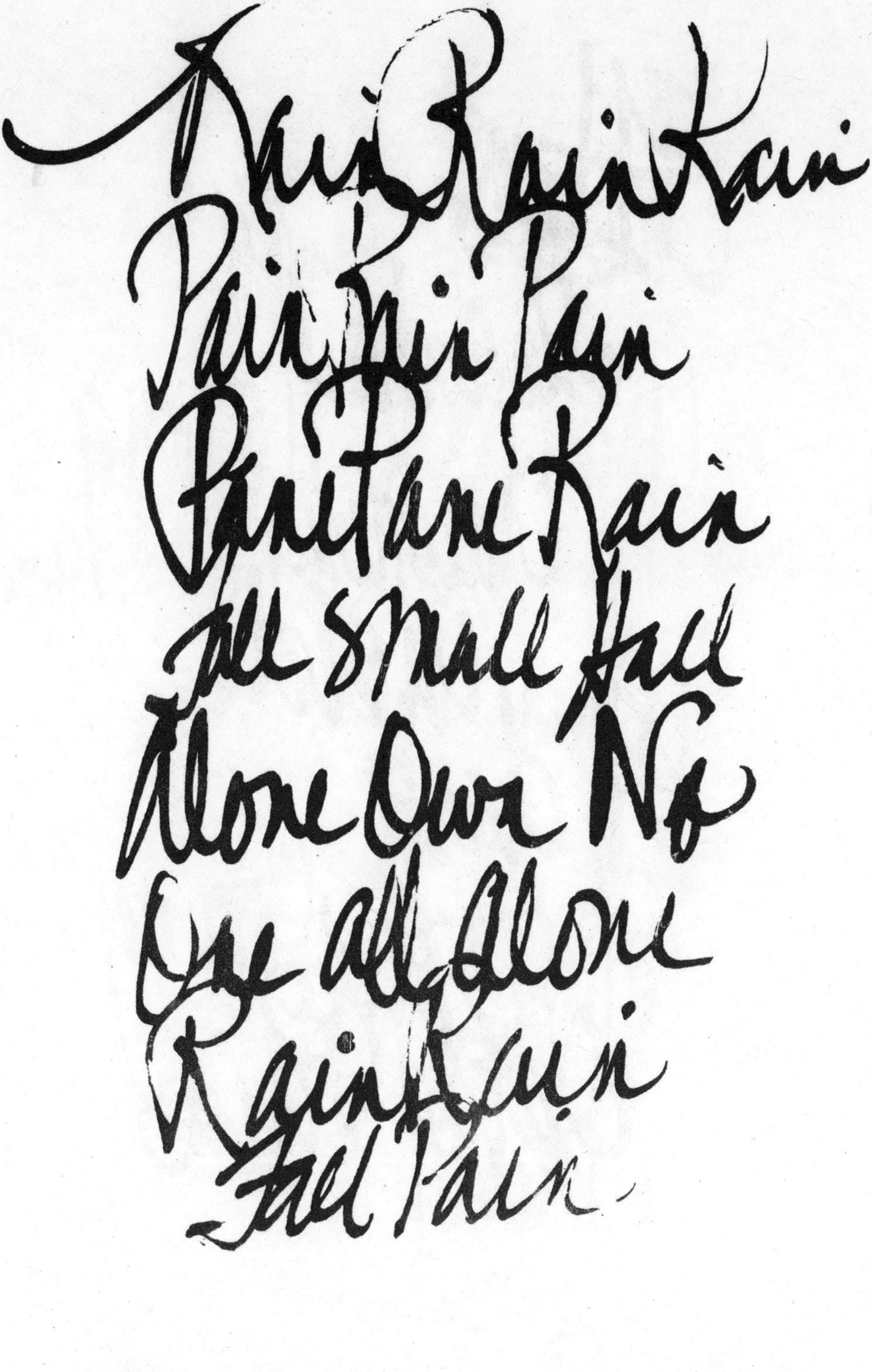

Rain Rain Rain
Rain Rain Rain
Rain Rain Rain
Fall Small Fall
Alone Over No
One All Alone
Rain Rain
Fall Rain

Hello
lowday
dawning
inside
A dark
Out of Pain

Another Order

Hello
Nowhere
NoTHING
Lightening
THUNDER
Tears
COME

Another Order

ONE BRIGHT LIGHT IN A DARK NIGHT

BRIGHT
FLASH
IN DARK
NIGHT
S.O.S.
SOMEONE
Hold ME
I NEED
WARM
FLESH

OH HOLD ME
I NEED
WARM
FLESH SOME
ONE TO LOVE
NOT ANYONE
BUT YOU WHO
EVER YOU MAY
BE COME TO
ME SOON PLEASE

Another Order

What do you do when you are alone? What are you like inside?

Who are you any way? Have you anything of use to say?

Another Order

why don't you
just
die
or go

who needs
you?

I do!

Then please
youre self
please!

Oh please
your self
please

and go easy

Soft Soap
and elbow
grease
after all it's only
your
own self
who Can Say

A shore
At last
reached

a home beyond
the dark
night sea
of rain

— Salty —

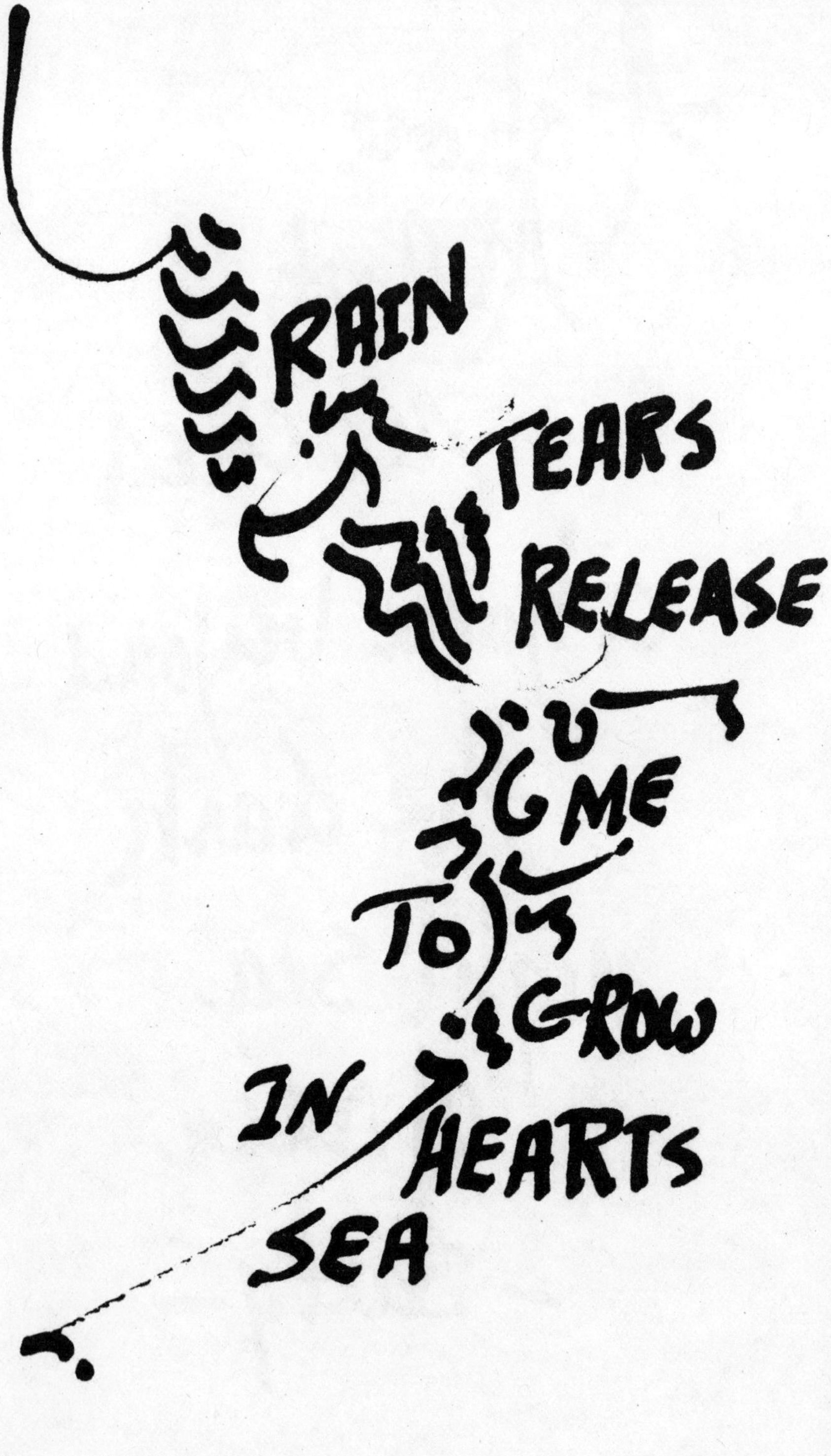

RAIN
TEARS
RELEASE
ME
TO
GROW
IN HEARTS
SEA

Release

1969

No:

No
I say
I don't have to play
games your way
I can play any game
I please
and still say
No

Yes:

Yes I say
I will play
your way
but don't hold
me to my
word any
longer
than
it's heard

Wild Flowers:

Would you
love me
if you knew
how many men
I had had?
Would you
feel sad?
Things are no
longer the same
Young girls
are changing
or were they
always
that way?

JC

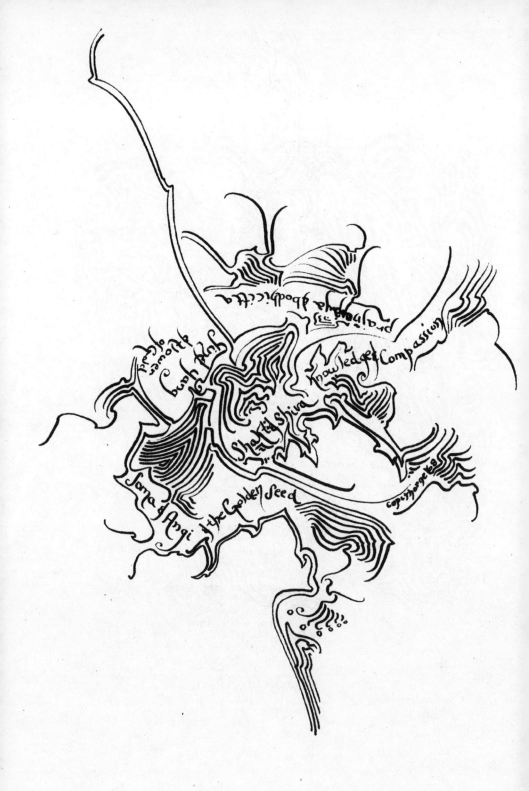

Little girl, you've become
a fuss budget
a worry wart
a harried
house wife
let it all go ... Let it
all go ... let go,
fly free

Another Order

There's another Order
to things
the order of the games
children play

of a doodle

of delight

produced from
my body of bliss
growing
beyond
my mind

There's another Order
to things
in which we
perhaps unknowingly

live

Should the outside
know the inside?

what frightens you?

Boredom
comes
from
fear

how boring!

you
know

Another Order

now that all life is impermenant
now that there is no real self
now that all is emptiness
now that none live
escape suffering
silence fluttering

46

Another Order

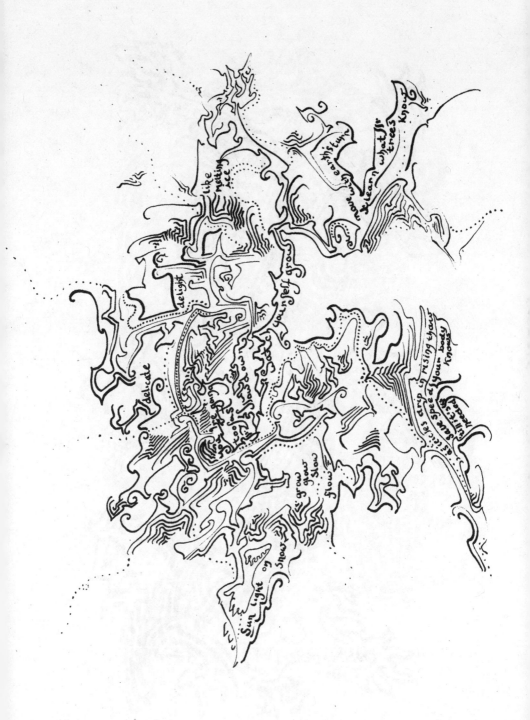

Nothing's expected

things keep changing

often a way out appears

unexpectedly

I don't know where it's going or what it'll be

Sometimes clouds clear

there's a path

Don't ask

But around here

there's a lot of rain

You never know

Another Order

World Dream

World turn
fire burn
light shine
colors come
sun gleam
grass grow
body glow
mind know
breath flow
muscles flex
nerves sing
life dream

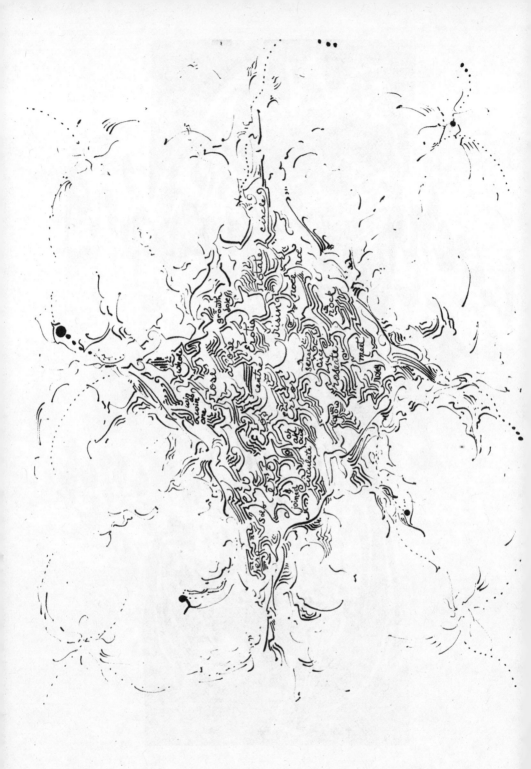

Another Order

Lucky Loving Longing Licking Lounging Looking Licking Life

from

Runes

1970

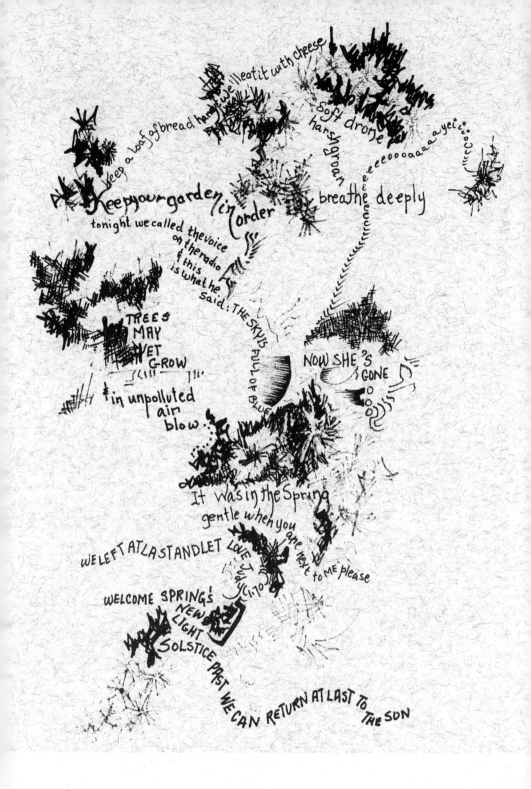

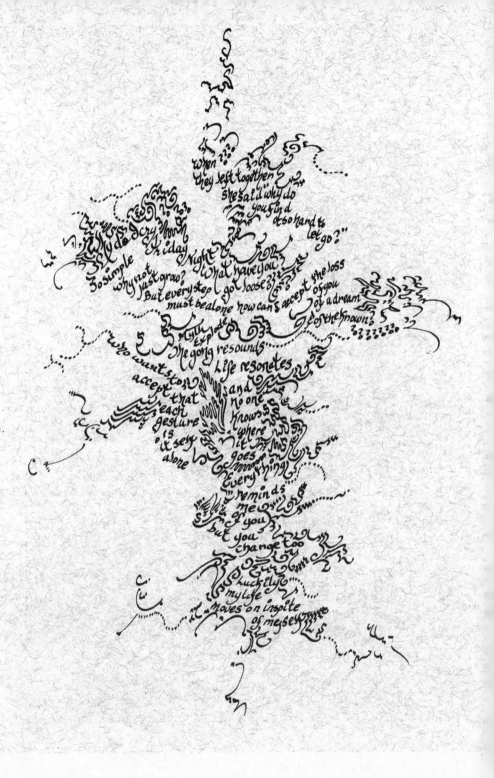

When they left together she said "why do you find it so hard to let go?" It's so simple Friday Night why not just grow? "What have you got loose? But every step must be alone now can't accept the loss of you of a dream of the known? Myth explode the gong resounds Life resonates and no one knows where it goes Everything reminds me of you but you change too who wants to accept that each gesture is itself alone luckily my life moves on inspite of myself

Riddle Song

geography of inland seas—

Does a love do more than find a goal?

There's that particular drone
driving home

mapping out the
wilderness
of the heart

Slow night
rolls by
how many
do we spend
alone & why?

watching the
word, the line
unfold
a story untold
Does a mind find out what the body knows?

an inner rhythm   laughs at me

texture of dream
of desire

velvet, fur, cross hatch
of sensation

JC.12.

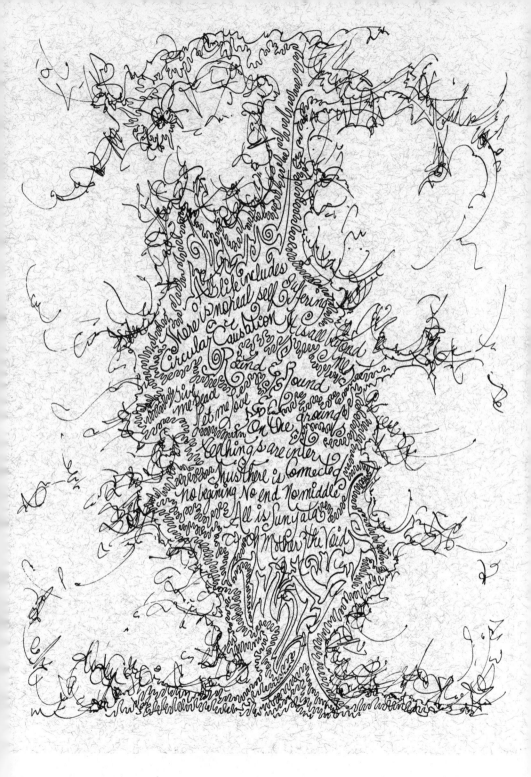

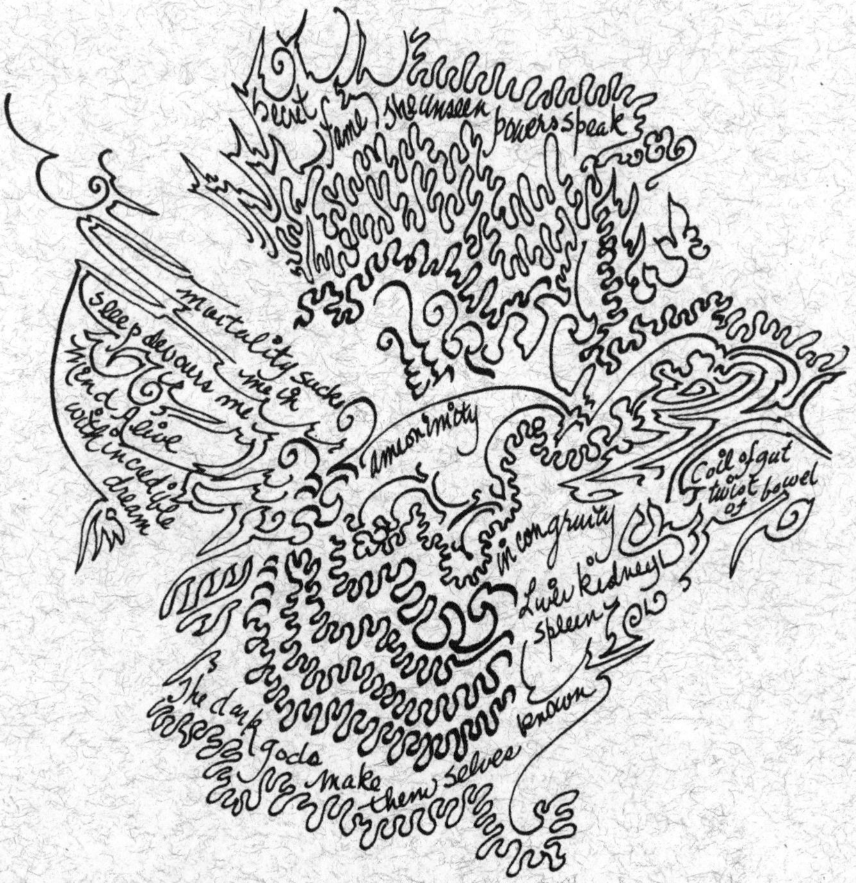
Secret fame
the unseen powers speak
mortality sucks
sleep devours me
mind alive with incredible dream
amour enmity
in congruity
Coil of gut twist of bowel
Liver kidney spleen
The dark gods make themselves known

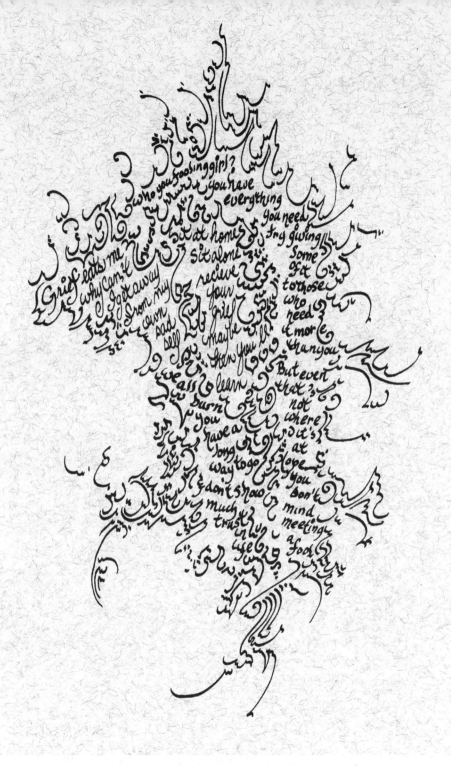

The Whole World Sleeps alone
Do their Dreams mesh
Spring
Springs
upon Tulip trees
us o Magnolias from the Deep South
Saxifrage
Burn Baby
& Many forms
The Whole World
of flox
grasses grow Samsara
green in Flames
down by the Sea
a Colt, furry eared Plum, Cherry
looks at me Trees flower
gently
Are our Dreams so strange? Tell Me what you see

Another Order

Start
Again
+ Again   Believe
        Move Me We
              are
              Wholly
              here
        that means you +
                      you
          wholly holy true

I like the songs children Sing +
                              Sing
        I love you

Some who be
        come like
              children
              become mad
              others grow
              old
                gently

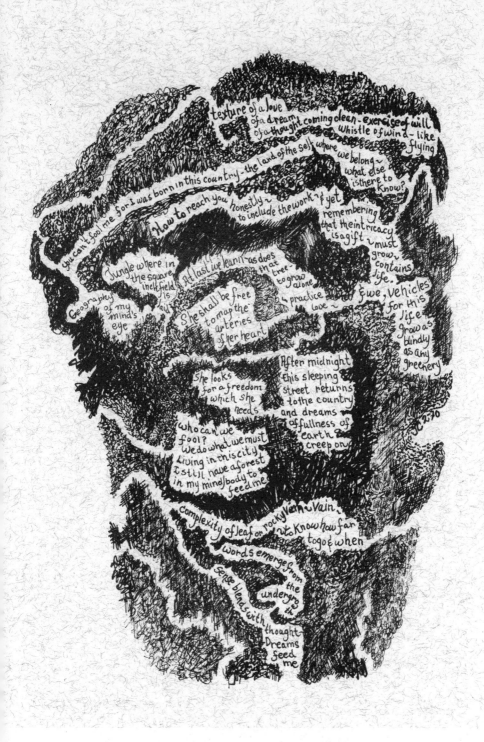

from

Miss Tree's Pillow Book

1971

CAT
JASMINE CURLED IN MY LAP

OUTSIDE SO MUCH SNOW. CINNAMON INCENSE BURNING.
CONSTANT FATAL FLAWS. SOME —NO—ALL— BALANCE OUT.
"IF I HIT YOU WITH A BIG ROCK OR A ROSE IT IS THE
SAME THING" THE ROSHI TOLD HIM TO TELL HER.

I LOVE YOU.

ALEX OUTSIDE SCRAPING WALKS AGAIN. WHAT WAS YOUR NAME
BEFORE YOU WERE BORN?

WE KEEP TRYING TO BE HUMAN.

RROTIC FANTASIES. SITTING IN THE GRAVEYARD ALL NIGHT.

ALIENATION OR ISOLATION.

THE LINE'S BECOMING CLEARER THESE DAYS. GINSENG
TEA HEATING ON MY GURNEY GAS HEATER.

 A GOLDEN SEED — A JADE PALACE — A HEART

AND A THUNDER BOLT

QUIET SNOW BOUND DAYS SOME BREATHS
PURE & THEN THE FEAR OF GOD.

WHO HEARS WHEN YOUR NAME IS CALLED?

JANUARY 17
THERE YOU GO AGAIN - HOOKED ON LOVE.
IN LOVE WITH LOVE THEY SAY.
WHAT'S POETRY - OR SONG? THE BREATH
OF SOME ONE YOU CAN NOT QUITE SEE.

♡

GOOD/ &
EVIL TURNING
       CHANGES MUST BE ACCOMMODATED
ON THE SUBTLETIES.

WITH PRECOGNITION   OF & CLARITY

                         PASSION

TO COME TO MIDDLE WAY.

ENERGY OF BRAIN ON HEART OF GUT,
OF CUNT OF LEGS CROSSED TIGHTLY
BRINGING IT TOGETHER WITH OUT
THOUGHT OR RATIONALITY.

WE KNOW WHAT YOU'RE SAYING & WELCOME
BUT ONLY SO LONG AS YOU KEEP ON
PLAYING.

USE IS IRRELEVENT TO THE FLAME.

ON AN ALTER OF GOLD
TRANSMISSION
FROM THE WHOLE GLOBE.

ACE HELLO.

DOWN TO THE BEACH TODAY
INSANE ECSTASY OF ROLLING BREAKERS
SALT WIND

MOUNTAIN TOPS HIT BY SUN
CLOUDS PILING UP FROM NORTH EAST

SUN COMING IN VERY WARM
INSIDE LIFE CONTINUES

JANUARY 17-

FORM SOMETIMES FILLING IN
SO ABSTRACT — HEN SCRATCHES ON
THE PAGE. CONCENTRATION. HERE
SECONDS SLIP BY LIKE TIRE WHEELS
IN THE RAIN. SOMETIMES THE FORM
BECOMES CLEAR & IT IS MAGIC MY
DEAR MAGIC SHEER FOR THE
CATEGORIES WERE NEVER THAT WELL
DEFINED.

THEN SUDDENLY LILA — MISS TREE
EMERGES

MEANINGLESSLY PLAYING
BEYOND THE PLEASURE &
PAIN
OH BEWARE
THE GAME

OPEN/CLOSE TO MY

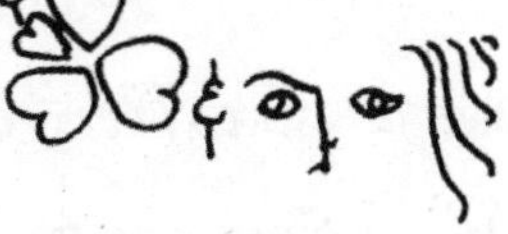

ESOTERIC BULLSHIT PILED SOME
WHERE ACROSS THE VALLEY FROM
WILLIAM WILEY'S LAND OF THE CLEAN & PURE

108 TIES

WILL MISS PLAYFAIR REMAIN HIS MISTRESS?
SHE WELL KNOWS THAT THERE'S NOTHING
SHE CAN DO ANYWAY. MAYBE YOU SHOULD
JUST IGNORE THE WHOLE THING.

SHE WOULD IF SHE COULD

BUT THE SPIDER'S WEB
ENGULFS US ALL.

          OH SOFT HE CAME & SOFT HE'S GONE
WHY CRY ABOUT ENCHANTMENT.
          BECAUSE THIS IS NOT JUST YOUR
SHOW.
          HIS WIFE'S BEAUTIFUL & HAUNTING
SOMETIMES SHE LOVED HER & SOMETIMES
SHE HATED HER GUTS.

THIS IS INTERNAL COUNTRY.

OF COURSE WE ALL KNOW.

TELL ME ART RAT WHO LIVES BELOW GROUND
YET LOVES THE SKY SO MUCH IT FLOATS
IN HIS HEAD LIKE A SILVER BOWL.
LATITUDE & LONGITUDE

CHARTING WITH A SHAKEY GOAL.

A LIFETIME DIEING TOO
            OF
            GETTING LINED UP.

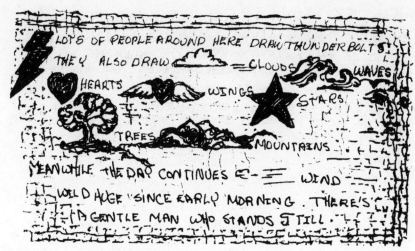

LOTS OF PEOPLE AROUND HERE DRAW THUNDERBOLTS
THEY ALSO DRAW CLOUDS WAVES
HEARTS WINGS STARS
TREES MOUNTAINS
MEANWHILE THE DAY CONTINUES WIND
WILD HUGE SINCE EARLY MORNING. THERE'S
A GENTLE MAN WHO STANDS STILL.

TRYING TO STRAIGHTEN OUT - CENTRE IN - BACK UNFOLD

BREATHE FREELY TRYING-
TYING

BOUND IN OUR GRACEFUL - BOUNDLESS
BONDS

KNOT
TIED LILA IN HER DANCE OF DELIGHT:

MISS TREE - mystery - FATAL FLAWS -

MANY BLUES - AZUL
AZURE
INDIGO
AQUAMARINE
VIOLET TOO.

WEST NORTH
THE LIGHT OF SUMMER SETTING SUN REMEMEMBERB NOW.

CHICKEN LOOKED UP AT THE HUGE FALLING PIECE OF SKY &
ASKED DO YOU LOVE ME? THE SKY REPLIED "THE MYTH OF
THE VAGINAL ORGASM WILL NOW BE RECIEVED". SO THEN THEY-
AS THE RADIO SAYS-CAME TOGETHER. THE GRASS & THE
TREE'S GREW BACK & WE WERE ALL RELIEVED. IT TAKES
ALOT OF WORK TO PULL IT INTO SHAPE. SOMETIMES
SHE WISHED SHE COULD BE DIFFERENT BUT THAT
NEVER WORKED

CARA'S TAPE ABOUT SLUG WAS FELT VERY STRONGLY

IT'S SNOWING AGAIN.

A LOT OF ELVES HOBGOBLINS & POLICE IN THE
WOODS.

SOMEDAY ALL THIS WILL BELONG TO THE MUSHROOMS
AGAIN.

OF COURSE IT READS.

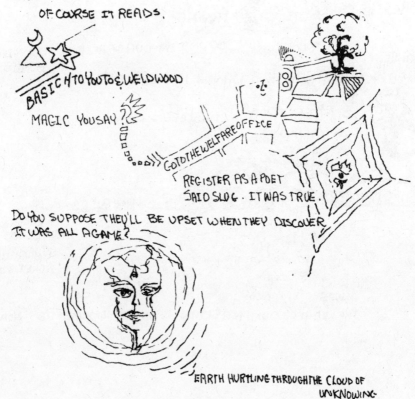

BASIC H TO YOU TO & WELDWOOD

MAGIC YOU SAY?

GO TO THE WELFARE OFFICE

REGISTER AS A POET
SAID SLUG. IT WAS TRUE.

DO YOU SUPPOSE THEY'LL BE UPSET WHEN THEY DISCOVER
IT WAS ALL A GAME?

EARTH HURTLING THROUGH THE CLOUD OF
UNKNOWING

MONDAY MORNING ~
    SITTING IN MY ROOM FULL OF ISELLIGHT. LIGHT FINE
TRANSLUCENT OPALESQUE PEARL & GREEN.

REFERENCE - SCALE - POSITION - RATIO'S

INSECT
TRUST
GAZETTE

WHY DON'T WE
DO WHAT WE
MUST TO BE?   SUPPERTIME ROLLS THROUGH. SNOW AT TIDE LEVEL

MIND'S SHATTERED. WHAT HAVE YOU TO GIVE? BE HAVE YOUR SELF.
HE RAN AWAY. WAS HE SCARED? ARE YOU A WITCH? SHE SHRUGGED.

JANUARY 21

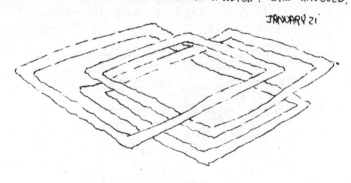

OH DEAR SAID THE BEAR: SHE BELIEVED ALL THOSE ROMANTIC SONGS
& LONGS FOR HER NIGHTS OF ECSTASY TO BE IN THE COMPANY
OF A MAN.
HOW LONG CAN YOU DO WITHOUT LONG? AS LONG AS LONG IS LONG.
RAIN DRIPPING DOWN GUTTERS INTO THE WET SNOW
  LIKE SHAKUHACHI OR KOREAN FLUTE
  SO YOU'VE HEARD THAT SONG? O.K. SLOW DOWN.

HERALDIC TABUZS!!

DONT LOOSE WOLY NEAT
VISITORS ALL DROPPING
IN & OUT FOR TEA &
THE LATEST DOPE
  HEARD IT THROUGH THE
  GRAPEVINE— DON'T FORGET
  SEE!
ARE YOU A MAGICIAN? MISS TREE
ASKED. DO YOU MEAN SLEIGHT OF HAND TRICKS? ASKED
HE. SHE WAVED HER HAND. YES, I GUESS I AM
HE REPLIED. LET US RESURRECT MYSTERY & ROMANCE
LET'S LET THE SEASONS RETURN TO FILL US WITH PLENTY
LET'S GET AS STRONG AS WE CAN BEFORE THE FALL'S
REALLY COME. ENRICHED REALITY.

RECYCLE THE FLAME

LONG JOURNEY THROUGH THE NIGHT. SNOW HEAPED UP INTO
PILES AGAIN. BUT BUT CARS SLICKING PAST & IT'S 60°
IN HERE THIS MORNING. MUST BE WARMING UP.
TRANSFUSSIONS OF ENERGY.
IT WAS A PLEASANT & VIRTUOUS EVENING I'M TOLD.
"KEEP THE MYTHS" HE SAID, INVOLVE YOUR SELF IN THEM
AS DEEPLY AS YOU WANT."
JASMINE BRING ESPECIALY TRANSLUCENT & FURRY.
"LETS SPEND ALL YOUR MONEY & RUN AWAY TO MAUI"
"GO JUMP IN A WHOLE."
"SO FAR TO GO."
"SOFT TOUCH."

VALENTINES DAY COMING UP.

WHILE I WAS ASLEEP MY WALKS WERE SCRAPED OFF.
VIOLIN MUSIC ON THE RADIO.

DECORATE MY MIND WITH ROSES
MY LIFE WITH SONGS & MAGIC
CELEBRATE WHAT'S HAPPENING
ITS ALL, DARLING THAT YOU'VE GOT.
TELL YOU WHAT I'LL LOVE AS LONG AS WE CAN STAND IT
& THEN OF COURSE WE'LL STOP.

LET US RESURRECT MYSTERY - HOLD IT LIGHT & HIGH - GOLD
BANNERS IN THE SKY

INSIDE A LAST THANK GOD I THOUGHT I'D NEVER GET
THERE SAID BEAR.

YOU WEREN'T THE LAST SAID ARTRAT NOR THE
FIRST BUT EVEN AT THE WORST YOU WERE THE MOST

"WHY DON'T YOU WRITE SPELLS" BEAR ASKED MISS TREE
YOU ARE A GOVERNMENT APPROVED POET?
"MADE IT" SHE CRIED "IN TWENTY FIVE EASY STEPS,"
"ETC."
OH FLIRI FLIRI FLIRI ROO I LOVE YOU A BUSHEL & WHAT THE HECK.
THE WHEEL OF FORTUNE SPUN THROUGH THE MAN WITH THE
ACE UP HIS SLEEVE.

BECAUSE HE WAS A MAN AT LEAST HALF THE TIME

NO WHISTLE NO ONE WHISTLE QUITE LIKE THAT
IN A SOFT WHEE.

MAGIC ~ SHEER DELIGHT ~ SO FAR TO GO ~ SO MUCH IN A LINE
AFTER MIDNIGHT ~ MORE STUFF FALLING FROM THE SKY ~ WHITE
LOVE LIGHT ~ SNOW BALL FIGHTS ~ DRAWN OUT INTO IMAGES
A HEART ♡ AND IN PALM OF

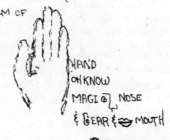

HAND
oh KNOW
MAGI @ NOSE
& &EAR & ☙ MOUTH

🌀 TO DO IN DESPAIR

WHO HAS TIME TO COMPLAIN? ─

RECYCLE THE FLAME

HELP

GAME NUMBER ONE

MAKE A NEW STORY AFTER
ALL THE SHAPES HAVE BEEN
SHUFFLED

DON'T
PUSH
THE
CHANGES

HE
SAID

SEE YOU
AGAIN

THE GOLDEN KEY

O.K.

THE
PLAY CONTINUES

─── TALLY ─── NO LOSS NO GAIN
NO WAY TO PLAY THE GAME EXCEPT BY TRANSMISSION OF MIND.

SPIRIT MOVING WHEN GRACE COMES THROUGH
IT'S OK YOU CAN GO NOW I WILL LIVE WITHOUT YOU.
SOME HOW THE TREES MUST BE SAVED
ALDER SPRUCE & YOU. I'VE BEEN GIVEN SO MUCH.

PEN UPON THE PAGE

SLOWLY

SKETCHES AS A BEGINNING'S MADE
ENTRE BARDO ONE
YOU'LL BE HOME SOMEDAY

JAN 18

SPRING STILL
COMING OUT

CHILDREN OUT AT
ALL HOURS PLAYING
LAST NIGHT & TRAFFIC
STARTED EARLY

TWO WEEKS AGO IT WAS NO CARS
AT ALL & TWO FEET OF SNOW.
THE BIRDS ARE COMING BACK TOO.

DOWN AT THE BEACH YESTERDAY
I ACCIDENTLY WALKED UP TO SIX FEET
BEHIND A GREAT OLD HERON

BLENDING
IN WITH
THE ROCKS
& WATER

OUT FURTHER
THERE FLOATED
A WHOLE GROUP
OF MERGANSER
DUCKS.
I TOOK PHOTOGRAPHS
MADLY.
A GREAT PLEASURE
RAN OUT OF FILM OF COURSE – JUST AS
THE BEST SHOT CAME UP.

WRITING, DRAWING ON TO THAT GREAT PASTURE AT THE
END OF THE MYTH OF ER. WHERE HAPPY MAIDS &
BOYS SPORT GENTLY, TRAILING RIBBONS, BRI
- GHT COLOURS IN THE AIR. SWEET INCENSE
EVERYWHERE.

Dumb of sublimity, produced by
sweet jollility, no lose or win.
Day ripped to shreds by anxious self. Angst, try
too hard, the nut cracked her shell none too
late. Dylan loves ladies, fire & ice.
Open secret for cyphering at will.
Our last long hill. When she goes it's with "PHAT!"
On her breath in an explosion through death.
♪ ♫ ♪ ♫ Decorative grid. Universal search.
Miss Stick's hunger's fierce, refined,
defined, indigo, ultramarine, wooed yet discrete.

Childish scrawl. Get beyond beyond, reborn.
Dark glamour beneath waves. Terrible,
the fear of nothing. Back to ground. Now.
Scrawl of soft confession "Didn't mean much."
Oh! Woe to us & our mixed identity.
Happens to us too. Just doesn't scan.
How to clear grid, start fresh, without blame.
Fresh air, breath of it, beyond fear, zero game.
Hello. Glad to know your name, although I
know it changes just the same. Your sad game
has caught me red handed blank eared. Green jacket
gold haired. BLAKE would certainly have had
his doubts. How true daughter. OH YES I taught
you to read between the lines. OH YES I
taught you to know. Friends COME AND GO, BREATH OH.
BREATHE DEEP. The new day's dawning. I wait for you, content
to know you'll come & so will anyone when they know not
how lovely they be be blowing in the wind ☺.
We are still often at war with each other
It eats my heart out daily. Snow now at noon
February 28 just afternoon.
Cars slush by. We reach the moon. Re-entry clear.
Cycle graphed. Pictogram. Welcome.

WHO KNOWS EVER WHEN TO START? ONLY THE GREAT WHEEL
TURNING THE STARS IN THEIR ESTUARY OF DELIGHT
WHILE FAR BEYOND THE WALL OF HEAVEN
MISS TREE MAKES HER RETURN INTO THE LAND
OF THE LIVING. SHE'LL START TO BUD
AGAIN ON VALENTINE'S DAY.

MEANWHILE THERE ARE TASKS TO ATTEND TO.
FRIENDS TO VISIT, WALKS TO MAKE,
CHILDREN TO PLAY WITH, CATS TO
CUDDLE; MUSIC TO PLAY YOU BY
EAR, FRESH AIR.
ALL BROKEN INTO AT LAST.

GO AWAY I SAID TO THE VOICE IN THE
HEAD YOU'RE A PAIN TO HEAR.

SO THE TWO BECAME ONE AGAIN,
MINDS MARRIED. TRUTH TO TELL
I KNOW MISS STICK WELL SAID
THE BEAR. THE MAN SAID THE
SAME THING. THERE IS NO
EXPLAINING EITHER MEN OR BEARS
THEY SIMPLY GO THEIR OWN MAD
DELIGHTFUL EXTRAVEGANT
SIMPLE DELICIOUS WAY.

BITTER BURNING WHEN LOVE'S GONE

A SPIRAL OF FLOWS

DISCOVERING DESTINY SHE HELD HERSELF STILL

CHILDREN PLAY IN THE STREET.

EACH YEAR IT BECOMES EASIER TO SEE

WORK WORK WORK MY MOTHER SAID

I WANT TO FINISH THIS BEFORE I DIE.

TO DISCOVER ANOTHER SIDE TO OUR
INSANITY

CAN YOU LOVE
& LET NO ONE KNOW?

DEATH FOR OUR DYING
LET THE LIVING LIVE

THAT THE RITUALS SPEAK WITH MEANING

THAT THESE WAYS ORDER OUR DAYS

THAT FIRE & WATER MEET

PHENOMENA
TURNING

THE TIBETAN PRINCESS LOOKED DOWN OUT
OF HER PALACE OF JADE & GOLD SHE TURNED
SUN INTO MOON & BACK AGAIN. REVERSING
THE CURRENT AS SHOWN.

I ALWAYS THOUGHT. ONLY BEGIN TO LEARN HOW TO STOP
SLOWLY THE DAY FADES. ALL WIND & BLUE AZUL. AZUR
& TOORQUOISE, YELLOW GREEN, DEEP PURPLE, ENBIGO
STRETCHING OUT THE COLOUR SCALE FAR FAR!
TO GO. A CHANT. A HUMM + A SONG

MONTHBY MONTH HOROSCOPE'S WEATHER & NEWS

1971
STAR FUCK
ASTROLOGICAL
CALANDAR

MARY LEE SATEN
Llewelly PUBLICITY

WHEN THE STORY TELLERS NO LONGER TRAVEL WITH THEIR
MINDS & THE POETS ARE AFRAID TO LOVE. OH THEN WE ARE
INDEED IN DEEP TROUBLE SO LET US FLOW AS FREE AS
THE AIR, AS DEEP AS THE SEA. WHEN I COME COME
WITH ME TO OUR HOME ON THE OTHER SIDE. SUR
ROUNDED BY BELLS & MAGIC TREES

MIND WANDERS THROUGH BLUE HAZE, JEALOUSY & DESIRE
BESET US IN THE MIDDLE OF THE DARK WOOD, TROUBLE
OUR MIDST AS WE WANDER AWAY.

BOREDOM ~ CURSE & GRACE OF GODS.
SOME SACRIFCE SLOWLY.
SAFFRON & MULTI-HERBAL BALSAM.
ONLY LOVE CAN BREAK YOUR HEART.
WHO CAN BE WHAT THEY ARE NOT?

THE GOOD FAIRY DROPPED BY YESTERDAY BRINGING MISTREE SOME
MONEY. FOR WHICH SHE THANKED THE DEAR GOD & SET TO
WORK BRASKLY.

TBEAR WORKED TOWARD THE DAY HE WOULD BE
FREE TO GO & GET MORE HONEY.

SUNDAY MORNING ~ FEB 1ST ~ TIDE SWINGING
BACK. MOON DID IT'S ASCENT AGAIN.
C.B.C. ANNOUNCES ANOTHER SPACE
SHIP HAS JUST TAKEN OFF.
NOW THE OPERA STARTS AGAIN.

GREEN VALLEYS ~ CITY'S FULL
OF PEOPLE ~ THE
SKY OUT SIDE
OPEN ENDED
BEYOND
THE RAIN.

GORDON PAYNES
PAINTING ON
THE SOUTH WALL

MICHAEL DE CORPEY
BOX

INTERNATIONAL
MOTORIST'S
CO-OP
CHAIR

THE VIEW FROM HERE IS WARM &
EXCITING. PEOPLE COMMUNICATING
AT LAST!

VISIONS OF RAINBOWS IN FEET SOLES

TRYING TO KEEP IT STRAIGHT SIR

UK.   A LOT OF UNEMPLOYMENT AROUND.

PEOPLE MOVING OUT - BACK & FORTH.

INTO THE COUNTRY AND BACK. BUT ON

THE WHOLE THEY ARE HAPPY SOULS

AND DON'T MIND THE PAIN.

IT'S ALL NOT AS STRANGE AS IT SOUNDS.

WE TAKES IT ANY WAY IT COMES.

THROUGH THE GRASSY GLADES WE TRAVELLED

AFTER THE STORM HAD CLEARED. WE TRIED

TO KEEP OUR HEADS STRAIGHT.

BUT THERE WAS LITTLE WE COULD

DO OR SAY.

NOT TO BE CLEAR THERE IS

NOTHING IN OUR WAY

ONLY OUR OVER-

WHELMING

DESIRE

TO BE

WHOLE

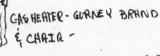

GAS HEATER - GURNEY BRAND
& CHAIR -

HEATER SENDING UP HOT AIR.

WHO SELDOM REALIZE WHAT DAY THEY ARE IN TILL FAR TO LATE
WHAT HAS BOTH SPACE & DURATION?
GIVE ME PHOTOGRAPHIC IMAGES OR EVEN LINE DRAWINGS.

ENCHANTED ISLAND EMERGING THROUGH THE RAINBOW
PROCENIUM ARCH.

EMBLEMS
OF ENERGY LIGHT A CYCLE NEVER BEGUN
    AN END TO DESPAIR
        HAVE WE COME THIS FAR? YES!
    YES YES   OH TOUCH GENTLY TASTE SWEET
WATER FEEL HOME.

ROUND & ROUND WE GO SAINT & SINNER   BARELY DARING TO FOLLOW
TO KNOW THIS GAME'S GOTO HOME & START AGAIN WITH THE
GOLD OF DETAIL SEWN INTO THE SEAMS OF YOUR GENTLE
JACKET. MOVE THROUGH THIS POROUS ELEMENT.

WHAT NEXT? HOW NOW SLEEPY BOW?
THE RAIN STOPS ~ WE WAIT FOR SUN.
  MID AFTERNOON HIATUS GRABS US IN THE GUT
WE UNDERSTAND THE IAM B's CLEVER PLANS
    KNOW THUS & ONLY TELL US CLEARLY SO
    THEN WEATHER FAIR OR THROUGH DARK FOG WE'LL COME
    CROSS WINTER'S BOW AND INTO SWEET SPRING BUT
REMEMBER ONLY WE ALL KNOW AND SING.

KALI~KARMA THE TIBETAN PRINCESS PUT ON HER
HEAD DRESS & WENT FOR A WALK DOWN YEW STREET
TO THE BLUE DEEP BAY. HEAVY CROWN OF GOLD WORKED
WITH PRECIOUS STONES. LUCKILY IT WOULD VAPORIZE
SHOULD ANY ONE LOOK OR SHE REMEMBER HER
IDENTITY.

NO SNAKE CHARMER TODAY. "A RELIEF TO BE SURE
MY DEAR."
ON THE BEACH THE FLUTE BOY IN HIS LOOK FOR GOTTEN
FUR COAT.

DEAR READER WHO DARES TO BRAVE THEIR OWN INSIGHT'LL
COME OUT WHOLE. AND WHO ELSE IS LEFT? WE'LL ONLY
KNOW THE DAWN & A SOFT SONG OF LOVE. SO GO DOUBT
LET US NOW GENTLY MEET IN THIS SPRING NIGHT.

BEAR WENT SEARCHING FOR HONEY. SUDDENLY HERE HE IS
INTO A GREAT FLOOD OF EMOTION.

MEANWHILE. REGINA TAKES A BOW. THE OLD COW.

OH YES SISTER SALVATION KNEW IN A GREAT BLARE
OF SAXOPHONE AND A GORGEOUS AFRICAN WALTZ.

NOT SIMPLE NOT COMPLEX OR AND BOTH. VISCOUS
THICK RICH STRONG WEAK RIGHT LEFT
MUST MUSK MUSTER NEITHER OPALESCENT
QUIVER RIVER STAIN STOP TOP UP PENULTIMATE
QUEST REACH SURE TRUE UNDER VANITY WHILE
XANDRA YOU ZEN ACTRESS BLUSH. COME DOWN END.
FEEL GRAPHIC.

Another Order

SO THIS IS TOMORROW TODAY.

HELLO SISTER WHAT'LL IT BE?

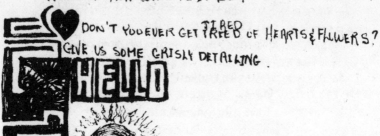

DON'T YOU EVER GET TIRED OF HEARTS & FLOWERS?
GIVE US SOME GRISLY DETAILING.

NEW DAWN @ 7:30 PM JANUARY # NO FEBRUARY 12TH
LEAKY FAUCETT DRIP # CINNAMON INCENSE @
SYNCHRONICITY CHECH.
GASOLINE ALLEY # RADIO # GRATEFUL DEAD
JANICE GONE.
MEDAL FLOW.
MAGICAL DOCUMENTS.
FIND A PERFECT PEN # GET THREE MORE SO THEY
CANDLE SSION

SIMPLICITY
ELEGANCE
FELL SWOOP
FULL SWEEP
MIDNIGHT SWOOPS
IBM
YES   NO
Z ABSURD
OD
CHILDREN'S BOOKS
THE FEAR OF GOD ~ BY GOD ~ GREAT
JUPITER

SO NOW YOU ALL KNO   THE CURTAIN GOES UP
IN THE COLONIAL
MAGIC
THEATRE

SO TODAY'S SUNDAY ~ VALENTINES DAY ~ OUTSIDE
THERE'S RAIN & CARS SLICKING PASSED
MILES DAVIS ON C.B.C.
EARL GREY TEA WITH FIREWEED HONEY &
LEMON JUICE LACED WITH GINSING.
NOW THE CHURCH OF PRICE OF AIR
PEARL OF GREAT PRICE ~ 159 ~
TUNE ~ THE WANDERER
HELD INTO PLACE BY THE LOTUS &
THE WINDOW PANE

YES YOU ~ WE ALL KNOW ~ HAVE TO GO
THIS WHOLE WAY ANYWAY

YOU ARE YOUR OWN GUIDE

WHY WORRY LITTLE GIRL? WHEN IT
ALWAYS WORKS INTO ANOTHER
DIMENSION BEFORE YOU ARE GONE ON

THE PAIN IS NO MORE OR LESS
THAN IT EVER WAS

DREAM IS OVER SAYS Mr. LEMON & WE JUST HAVE TO
CARRY ON . TRUE ~ FALSE ANYWHICH WAY? WHO DUN
IT & WHERE ARE WE GOING ANYWAY?
MADNESS CREEPS OVER THE LAND . WE ARE STILL
ALONE AFTER A LONG DAY . PEOPLE PAINTING SEA
SCAPES AT THE BEACH

MISSTREE
WITH HEARTS
IN HER HAIR

DIAMOND
BODY IN
MISSTREE'S

DO THE SIMPLEST POSSIBLE THING IN THE MOST
DIFFICULT (OR VICE VERSA) WAY .

MISS STICK LIVED WITH A LOFT OF DARK FEATHERS
OVER HEAD . MING'S A SOFT FURRY PUPPY . ROSIE'S
A SKUNK .

GIANT SOFT FURRY MEMORIES FROM GUT & TONGUE
CIRCULATION OF MIND THROUGH CHANNEL OF
NERVE & BLOOD . THE WORLD WHIRLS ON, ONLY
OUR PLANS HOLD US BACK .

REFRAIN: HERE AGAIN SANE & FAIR &
             FULL OF FORTUNE'S SHAME .
HE IS LIKE WISE MOUNTAIN . ROCK HOLD
FIRM . SHE'S QUEEN INVISIBLE MOON
SHEEN . HOLD THE OPAL FIRM   BLUE FIRE
GLOW . TOURQUISE LIKE BEACH SHALE THRU
SNOW .

MAGIC MY DEAR ~ SHEER MAGIC ~

THE NEXT DAY WE CONTINUED IN THE SAME MODE. NOT COMPLAINING.
OPEN SESAME ~ SESAME SAKS DELICIOUS IN YOUR FOOD.
JASMINE SITS ON THE STOOL NOW   CHANGING BACK & FORWARD
FROM DEMON INTO CAT.   SHE WANTS SOME OF THAT FANCY
TUNA CAT FOOD THIS WEEK   BUT SHE CAN EAT BROWN
RICE TOO.

DOCUMENTING
UNCONCIOUS
PROCESS

FOR A LONG TIME IT HAD ALL BEEN HEARTS & FLOWERS GIVING IN JOY & SHARING
SOME GETTING TOO.   THANK YOU. BEARS GET HONEY.

Short hand please. Who's got time for else?
Rain outside. Rattle of tambourine on radio.
Kept within human bounds. Did best we could
Sister. Slipping, sliding through reality.
Read black on white. Grey scale. Greatness a
singing sign of some relaxation.
Oh gentle crotch in apple tree.
JUXTAPOSITION OF YOU & ME.
It's nice to read totally. When did you loose your
face, faith? Did you stop growing? Traveling
light. Need of music from which words
come fruitfully. Now it reads you. No stop or
start only movement inside or out.
We are afraid of nothing. That little death. Cree,
Haida, Beaver, Bear, walnut tree. Images
growing on the grid. Some form of regularity. So,
form of sense. THEMIS, SOPHIA. Enough of that. Join
me, if that's your pleasure, need, desire. Surely learn
is need. Over & here, any where. What about good
music & bad what about high wide handsome man.
Careful please there's more to do yet, & pain's a reality.
Stop & start. ♡ . Even little boys playing trucks in
mud do that (& play in mud that grown up the tree).
That grow up a tree & shine like silver water.
Fill the jade palace with air. sun & fresh straw.
Even the rain's today.
Today: silver slivered (Keiraku) nerve ends. Breath
still to be let in & out or grown into today. Again. Refrain
today. Slippery dream/reality gestalt caught in shoulder.
Jasmine greets you. Welcome & Surprize, all roads lead
to the same place. The steps go as far as they can
then gently, on your own you cross to another shore.
Beauty's in my mind to find in horn & flute.

It's so easy it's hard to believe. Move to it, meet half moon, half sun. If you doubt it's 7:30 Am February 24 a man you know just died. We all know but how or why? Don't ask for a roaring meets the ache in my head. I've gone as far away as I can today, the wise woman said. Sand dune, sea bright blue. Strange, more than real ships. How to be dead on?

Who reads? Only sea gulls, crocuses and maybe bears.

February 24: Miss Tree siezed her pillow book when she woke up. But the wind had already whipped away her dream. Incredible blue sky. Terror of west wind across empty spaces beaches & parking lots like a prarie Chinook & that's what it could be if it only warmed up. She though she should look for a bicycle if she only could get out the house. A clarity today which is hard to match in mind. Out at the renowned U.B.C. they take pictures of children while they listen to the songs of whales.

Wind howling round the block. Nemesis. An absurd reliance(!) reliance on a new life.

Cold, cold, we are all getting cold & old.

Today is Somebody's BIRTHDAY. And we are participating in whatever way our minds drive us.

BLUE, BLUE. RIPPLES, WAVES. WHITECAPS.

"You're wondering about Something & I'm wondering about nothing." He said. "People are amazing." Truely amazing, cruely amazing. Close to my heart, like soft goo, goe as Matty calls it.

So at last, at little last I can hear you.

Jung says that the magic marriage is never a stable one. The archaic crafts, subtle nuances, arts are dimming although we now have a renaisance in many areas.

Good bye Love, gold bird in silver tree sing electronic Bach while this wind howls rough as any element scorned and raging.

Fierce through door jamb, window mold, cross radio beat, invading inner heat, go, slower.

How to get on with it. Did, do you think you choose? Pulse
chart. Gram of breath. To be, being , pain/pleasure gain
AC/DC Any analogy. Stop & go.   Rose
windows, an old Dodge. Blue Volkswagon , sun roof
will open, should rain ever go.
Back to centre. 12 o'clock Noon. Last week in February.
Abortion of mind. Time to Kill. The same story through all
time. Past time now caught in spines shining. See Velour,
see, soft, feel. Touch of genius. Touch of sensuous waif.
Children look in for a new home. Bodies in the Benares
end of the Ganges. Childish adoration. Canned heat.
Sirens wailing. White sound.
Withdrawl. Shit. Shsh said Sage's mother. Sage is five
and friendly. He likes mud & has a fraternal bear.
His hair is orange & he'd like to marry Kyo but's
afraid he's too young. She's seven & goes to school
seldom.
Shortly & is the name of the outdoor cat.
Kundalini is Asian Sometimes before you remember.
Earth & the rest & hit the ground.
Brakes squeal in the continuing rain. Woe unto us (1000) one
thousand times.
Enter into the forest. Feel easy. Soft touch.
Having to stand on one's own feet. Keep memory clean,
flute, oboe, tambourine, drums. Being deep through
ecstasy

MYSTERY floats high above rain
clouds, grey, on wings of gold giving
off prismatic glints of electricity.

Stars flashing ~warm stars bekoning ~ bright light ~
only follow the rain ~ let us move you into new deb...
us sing sweet & clean

Say what you like, believe, make such saying worth a listener.
Say it with love. True.
Mad Jasmine rushing through from out of doors.
Skid up, forceful hello. Don't scatter wool.
Spent morning rewinding skeins. Cat's cradle
duck soup, wild goose, no monopoly on pain.
We all have hurt, & pleasure seduces us. Featherd
owls in midnight trees, seeing straight
into ourown hearts. Dead centre again.
Dumb old owl in black night tree come to me.
"Hurry, hurry," A voice crys. Who? Why? How?
Try to be? Try while wind grabs us dumbly.
Arc of nerve, pile of aggregates, family.
We're all part of this great heap, flesh & dreams.
We all find each other miles away. Oh!
Who knows what we'll do, some how must see you.
Squeal of breaks. Do I need you? You are wind.
Elements make your corporal sensual
being. You run mercury through my veins.
Mad glamour of rage torn waves, olive green.
Salt fold in wind, wave tops, white caps, for cream.
Cold pierce spirit's layer, run wild children's
glee, fallin water, feel red & burning.
Catch a water bird died in flight, tide-
carried into rocky shore. Kitsilano
Point become a central mysterie.
Nde night light, day's glory, we remain empty.
We remain embossed by lightening
on convoluted brain singing blues.
Shame! Marriage a sacrement not a name.
Rain on thought & sense, amber flower, sweet
pea. Beyond doubt into prarie sunset.
Willow spring. Try getting beyond our games.

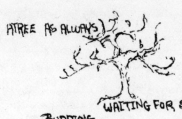

A TREE AS ALWAYS

WAITING FOR SPRING TO START
BUDDING.

THE OCEAN WAITING FOR THE WIND TO
START WAVING

THE WIND FORMING INTO CLOUDS
WITHOUT WAITING

THE
MOUNTAINS WAITING

ALL THROUGH TIME KNOWN

THE SUN SHINING FROM
BEHIND

THE MOON RECYCLING

HELLO OUT THERE. COMING IN CLEAR
THANK YOU. COME AGAIN.

TENDER NIGHT FALLS INTO SPRING'S EARLY DAWN
WIND, TIBETAN PRINCESS IN YOUR SOFT HAIR
SAVES MOSS FOR YOU TO CURL UPON. MYST'RY
OF RAINBOW CONTEMPLATION UNDER WILD
ARBUTUS LIMB OR CEDAR BOUGH · BIRDS FLY
NORTH, AN OPENING OMEN. CONSIDER ROSES.

VITIMANS MINERALS, SILVER & GOLD
COLD SPRING'S WIND SKY BRIGHT BLUE IN WEST SEA SPLASH
AND MURRMUR. BIRDS OUTSIDE LIQUID TRILLING THROUGH
OLD WALLS. AUDIENCE & SHOW ALTOGETHER NMOW
LISTENING TO WHITE LIFETIME RADIO
TRY TO BE ANY WAY ELSE BUT TRUE BLUE.

PROPORTIONS OF LUST, PSYCHE TIED IN TO CUPID'S
LOW LOVE BOW NO WAY TO LET GO.
AMBER, SAFFLOWER OIL, PRAWN'S SAUTEED GOLD
& ROSE. SEA GREEN, ABSURD GRIS GRIS SPELL. WELL
ASIDE FROM THE MINOR PAINS OF LIFE THINGS ARE GOING
SWELL. FUK YTH PULSE BEAT ENG
FORGOT MA

FALL
DOWN
& WE DO TOO
INTO ILLUSION
WHI SO FAR GONE INTO THAT
BLUE. TELL ME DADDY
WHAT SHALL I DO
I'LL NOT GO MAD
LOOSE MYSELF UNDER
THAT BELL
HOW TO CARE FOR THE
CHILD ~ CHILDREN GROWING
LIFE
NOW
DEATH & OUR VAIN
"ATTEMPTS TO "KEEP IT
UNDER CONTROL" 
THE WORLD WHICH GOES
ROUND & ROUND ~ LEAVING US WONDERING WHAT
WAS GOING DOWN & ~ WHAT WE JUST HEARD
GAY LIBERATION WITCH ~ HEAVY
POLITICAL OVERTONES
AS IF WE
SETTLE COULD
OUT
HOW NO
TO BE ONE
MORE KNOWS
CLEAR? WHAT'S GOING
GOOD THATS TO HAPPEN NEXT.
SCRAMBLE JUST WHAT WE
THEY PUSHED WANT.
BARDO & ON PAST THE LAST
THAT THIS DISCOVERED
IT'S WAS HOW
BEEN ALWAY
NOW. IT'S UP TO YOU NOW IT'S UP TO YOU
SAID A VOICE FROM
WORLD'S END. PERCHED JUST
OVER MY SHOULDER SOFT
GENTLER THAN I'VE EVER
KNOWN TEMPTING.
LET US MEET.
AS MYSTIC PASSED THE MAD WIFE'S
HOUSE IT STARTED TO RAIN. THEY
SEDUCED HER WHEN SHE WAS VERY
YOUNG & I DID NOT REALLY
KNOW WHAT WAS
GOING ON. SAD
SONG WORLD
ON TOO
LONG
HELLO
NICE TO
KNOW YOU.
WELCOME
TO THE OTHER
SIDE WE'VE
WAITED AND NOW YOU HAVE COME. END.

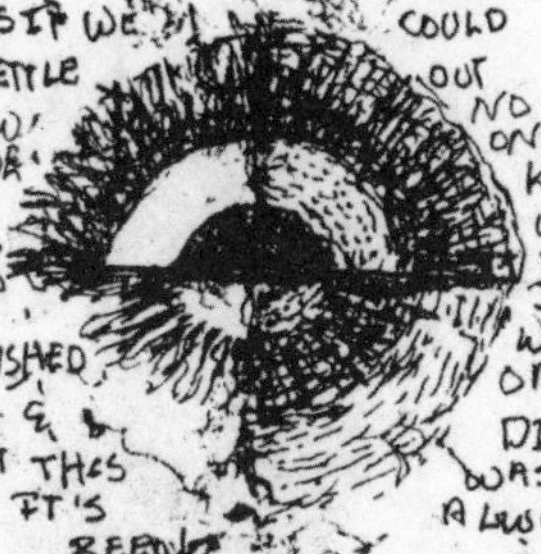

VIBRATION
AMPLITUDE FLOW
RUSH O STOP GO FEEL
SUNSHINES NOW LIGHT
NONE FOOT FELL LAST NIGHT
MOTHER MAN
SAXIFRAGE
TRANSITION'S
CHANGES
CENTURED
DOGWOOD CALYPSO GWORT
INHERENT
SOLOMON'S
SEAL

FIRST : This morning's sun ☀
February's last day but one
Snowed one foot through night
Snoveling continues. Peace ☮
Fridge humms. Hmmm. Neck informs of doubt but
feel the warmth of sun.
Magic taugh this orb love & it seeps like honey
into twisted tiss-ue no seam bound by
any more than itself into selfless shroud. No
death by crowd. Instead don't the sun go. This magic
hour will return but will you
"Know how?" "The best way I can & help of friends."
A genetic code which must befound. Fresh coffee
Snow melting building's shadow swallowing
my hand in its cool swell as dark follows
light, swell old sun!
Oh who wouldn't? So far & near will it come His way
again? A familiar refrain! GLOSSALIA · Ganglia 'ion.
Raising raisin & nut bread by the Gurney's gas
heat. Madrigals on C.B.C. Water tap turned up
stairs. Rush in pipes & drips in kitchen sink.
New day dawns & holds strong. Content, know you'll
come as will all who know not to do but
be sweet sea salt personification
of Kali/Arabras, two become one.
Images racing outward through stars. Solar
power create coronas of prismatic
light, centerd locii of energy.
Snow much melted. Dinnertime.

Another Order

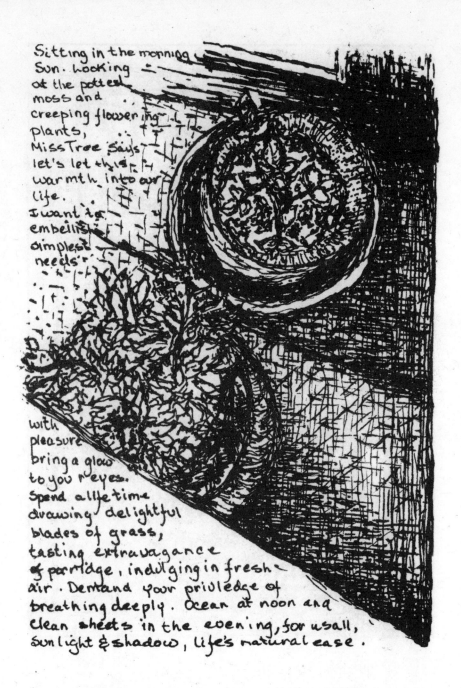

Sitting in the morning
Sun. Looking
at the potted
moss and
creeping flowering
plants,
Miss Tree says
let's let this
warmth into our
life.
I want to
embellish
simplest
needs

with
pleasure
bring a glow
to your eyes.
Spend a lifetime
drawing delightful
blades of grass,
tasting extravagance
of porridge, indulging in fresh
air. Demand your privilege of
breathing deeply. Ocean at noon and
clean sheets in the evening, for us all,
sunlight & shadow, life's natural ease.

SUN
SOFT
MORNING
GRASS
GROWING

BREATH
FLOWIN
WARMTH
CAT   CLOUD
NAPPING

Another Order

Saint Patrick's Day: Miss Tree met Sea Witch
who was wearing green. They embraced each other
and continued on their charming way as ladies
who know each other & themselves do. Without, or
beyond, jealousy whatever the stakes. And stakes mean
less the closer we get to the heart of the matter.

Lifetime radio reported weather to Magic Bear. Who
listened also to the stock reports.

Jasmine curls up, licks her right front foot, finished,
head down, eyes close, dream, colours swarm, rug soft,
warm. Hello come in Space Patrol.
Even break. Let fire & water meet.
Earth & air happy, together. Living sweet songs
out, open & free.

Open field, bounded by conifer juniper & yew.
Bagpipes can be heard behind that distant morain
& glacier peak.
Wind, waking up, breath coming through.

Yes a child concieved of sun & moon
Air & water. Conceived only in full
Knowledge. Body & mind, two together,
Beauty & beast combined.

Mirror of each other, interface,
peat moss & roses, spirit & soul joined.

Down to water's edge. Ocean slapping on rocks,
a magic place. Transforming doubt into love,
fear into positive energy. Clouds built up
high in western sky. Shades of blue every-
thing, layer of cloud on cloud, sky, mountain,
hill, tree. Ocean in rows of tiny repeating
waves. Birds on the sea. Ducks duck under
the blue, grey, green. Little tails flip up as head
goes down in joyous gesture of whole body.
Beige sand scattered with silver and grey
and constant blue again of muscle shell,
rocks & pebbles of granite blue grey.
& all the time lap lap goes the sea, slap
lop go the waves, sending up ripples of
peace to please & lull me. & a deeper
green streak appears in the water as a
wind stirs it up bringing in further briney
refreshing smells. Little bits of foam stir along
the slip slapping shore gently, cold. Fingers
feel the breeze biting. There's fresh snow
on Hollyburn where the sun cuts through
the clouds, illuminating, spring, brilliant,
cold, late coming. People line the beach
in quiet company. Two St. Bernard puppies
gambol on the grass. A young man in a
purple jerkin sleeps in branches of an alder
tree. Look at the strange bird! The puppie's
master says to me. Sea weed, kelp & sea
lettuce lie in mind cleaning salad at my
feet. This grey-silvered, infinitly grained
old log well holds me. The earth recieves, frees.

After realizing there's no way to get ahead or behind.

Getting things into perspective

Spring's birthday. Full of white light

Another Order

from

Arrangements

1973

March 21

This is spring, the day & month of return.
Meanwhile we pray to awake in another way
When man, woman & child can help each other.
Green tree in the doorway... we are...
Amazed by gifts... generosity...
vision... sobered by tasks...
trials to be run...
we have not yet begun.

Oh it is the equinox of the rising
Song of the sun.
Children pass...
We know what
we should do...
& there is still
joy in this
selfish
mind.

Somtimes, a lover
blesses us

Marrow of fire,
arc of light,
within the
helium laughter...
You have to burn
to be born in the sun
This is spring...
bursting beyond logic...
Singing a song to the
winds of chance & this
Sweet... bitter sweet... fluid delight.

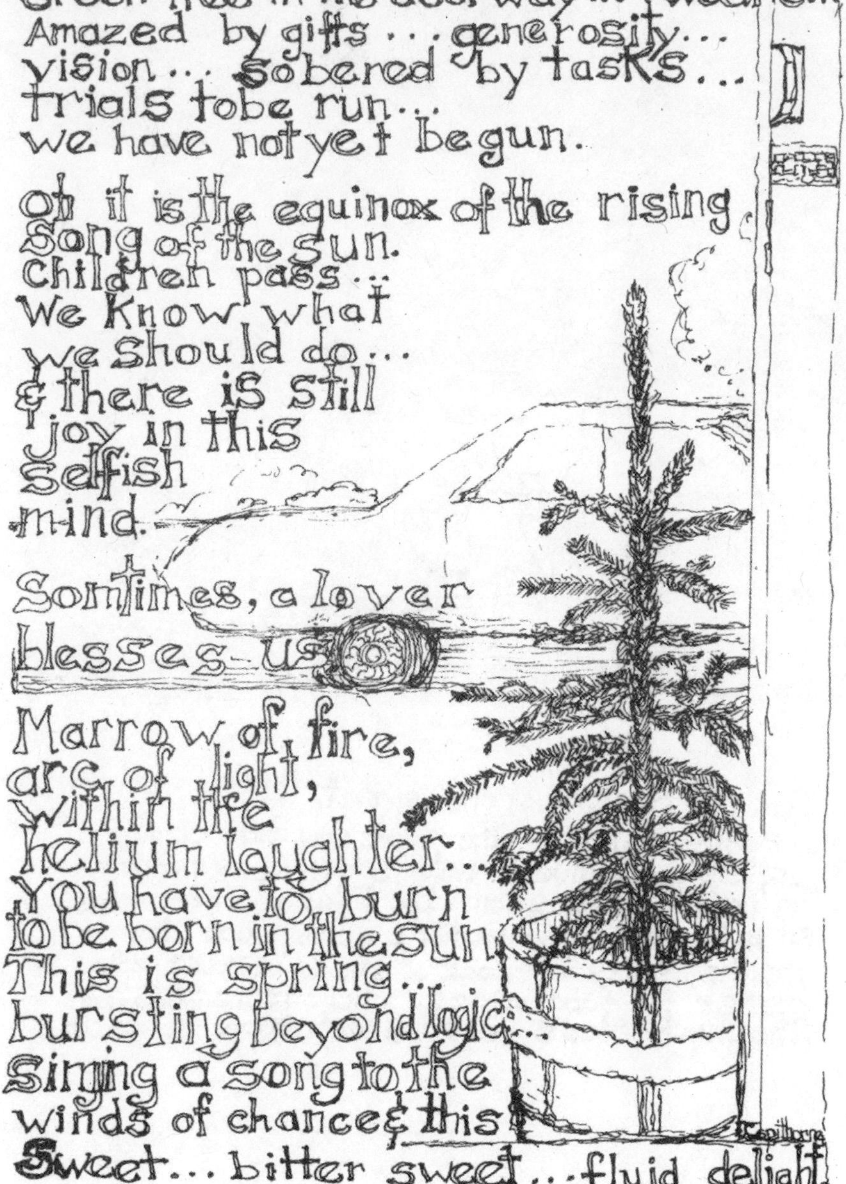

Pyramid Rock, just after sunset.
Cut poles, gentle on the swede saw, tide comes
up, seagulls dive for water, splash, any moment,
as usual, friends come by. Piled alder branches
sit in heaps around water's edge, wood chop
thunks of axe at back of shed, in house dishes
clatter for food, voices, where is the white gas?
The chuck slaps around feet, supper serves us.

Yes of course
we must be
careful
which words
continue,
what
we
need

Each sings
their own song.
Night continues.
You feel good to me.

Water runs. Rain down
drain, past the glow,
windows and doors, the glass of
which like shoji screens, holds
while Dylan sings.
And the night continues.
I leap up and embrace you
long after you have gone.

Another Order

Rose bush, Plymouth &
Olivetti each equally
lovely in morning's
Sunny garden light
leaping off multiplicity
of incredibly green
grass blades

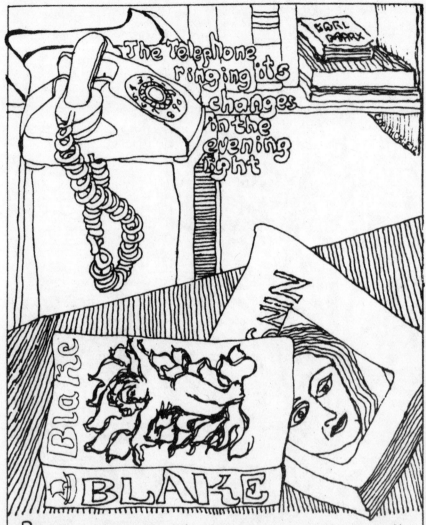

The telephone ringing its changes in the evening light

KARL MARX

ZZZ

Blake

BLAKE

Rain on the roof all night long cleaning my mind with white sound. Do you know I am waiting for you? Will I tell you that when you get back? Who does not know how much easier it is to dream than live?

And then it finally was worth it all. It all comes true. Overwhelm them with paradoxes

Inside, fluttering, I can feel you.

Time to begin again. That these things: bicycle, plant, chair, gentle cat, symbols of inner goal, supply their own light. Omens of wind, cold spring bite, knowledge that nothing lasts.

Stop:
move into
being time:
before it's too late
Dreams die:
shattered by day.
Pray for that art
which may grow
again from
shattered parts.
Sun coming in from
South-west: future
a chasm, past dreams
gone, this present best.

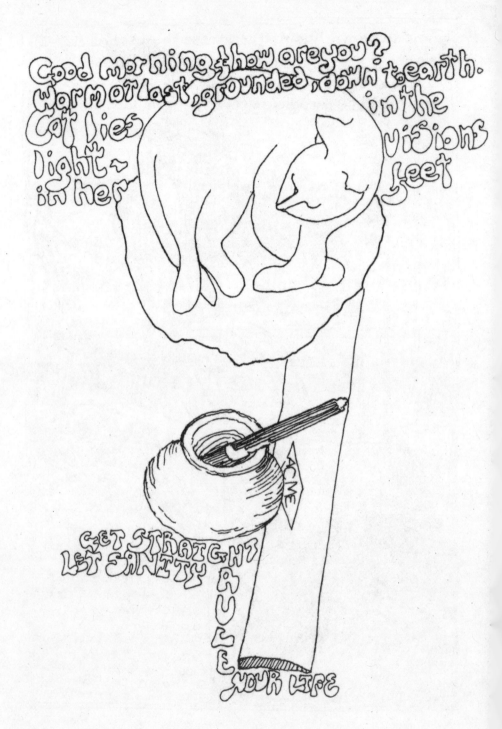

Good morning, how are you?
Warm at last, grounded, down t'earth.
Cat lies   in the
light ~   visions
in her   feet

GET STRAIGHT
LET SANITY RULE
YOUR LIFE

Another Order

COME ON,
LET IT OUT
LET IT OUT!! GIVE A SHOUT
THEN LET IT FLOAT on the river...
live
inside.
DO YOU?

She didn't know what came next... couldn't guess...
still the silver Moon rang the changes made by love...
Nobody knows the truth...
...only what they, them
selves,...

Must do.
Meanwhile it is spring... flowers are in bloom
Oh go slow in to the soft air...
As he left, he gently touched her head...
Lightening, thunder, when he goes...
At last, fresh breaks the storm.

Some people want clarity & some people want style & some never really know what is happening...

It is a slow day

Now what does there now?

Who goes it

She stopped, shook

Herself...

SLOW
SLOW...
Now start again darling...
Now start again darling...
Now start again

Slowly
No one knew what to do
Nor dared say they were sorry

Another Order

THE KEYCHAIN OF EVENTS

FLYING HEART

HELLO WELLCOME TO

THE IMAGE NATION

VISION PATROL

Another Order

WINTER
MOON:
SUMMER
SUN

PATTERNS
TRANSLATING
BODY/MIND

CARROTS & CEDAR
COOKING
FUN

BRIGHT
BANNERS
IN THE SUN
A DAY OF
TRUCE CALLED
FOR FRIENDS
PEACE WON

Sun out side the morning window sometimes breaks
through clouds, strikes my eye. Last night:
wanted to bring you something; had nothing to
give. It was empty; blue, black & green. Moods,
unpredictable, sweeping down off mountain
range, high, indigo, fierce.
Lucid wind
ripples sea
aerates dreams!
cool evening blows in. Bright gold leaves
in evening shade
glimmer through
remembrance
of what we
could be.

& Now
Good
Morning.

To love without attachment
you (each) ask this of me:
that which I avoid
(for how long before
the seasons decay us)
& the efforts:
fuel to feed the fires
we are burned by... & then
To say: please wait, & then
when it is over! To know
how to leave

Another Order

We always knew
what we should do,
what we did
was not enough.
the world runs down
in its sea of blood,
the dying call
to us and we
can barely love.
What use to tell
the pain of knowing
when those who listen
have heard too much
and those who don't,
encased in their steel
bones, their hearts
ticking out hours
of meaningless lust,
refuse to hear,
watch bodies burning
with glazed eyes,
untouched.

THE HOLOCAUST
CONSUMES

THE SIGNATURE

THE EYE
SEES

And blood poured down,
the colour of roses in the evening light...
run all your life from violence,
& some day chaos collides.

The night is coming...
We go down, metal exploding in guts
to the smell of excrement...
no wisdom can describe our eventual death.

Oh they came to us with love & found hate,
fearful greed, defoliation,
mass slaughter, poisoned skies,
bodies changed beyond recognition,
a never opened mind.

Where could we ever go to hide?

April 19

What we have done then,
was the best we could do.
There should be more...
will be,
since all things change,
and continue, also.

Albion's Rose Blooms to Calypso Beat

1985

Before my eyes cherry blossoms open
In my ears silence sings
A remembered rythm pulse thru blood
Love cry sin sustaining flood

Victories of sense over doubting mind
pleasure should run unconfined
like water down forest hill
Until at last, I am patient & still

Spring comes in and carry me
Spreads soft wing give holy ease

O I have a
long way to go O
For I am alone
and far from home
Since my true love
left me
Under the jilting
Under the tree O
jilting tree.

144

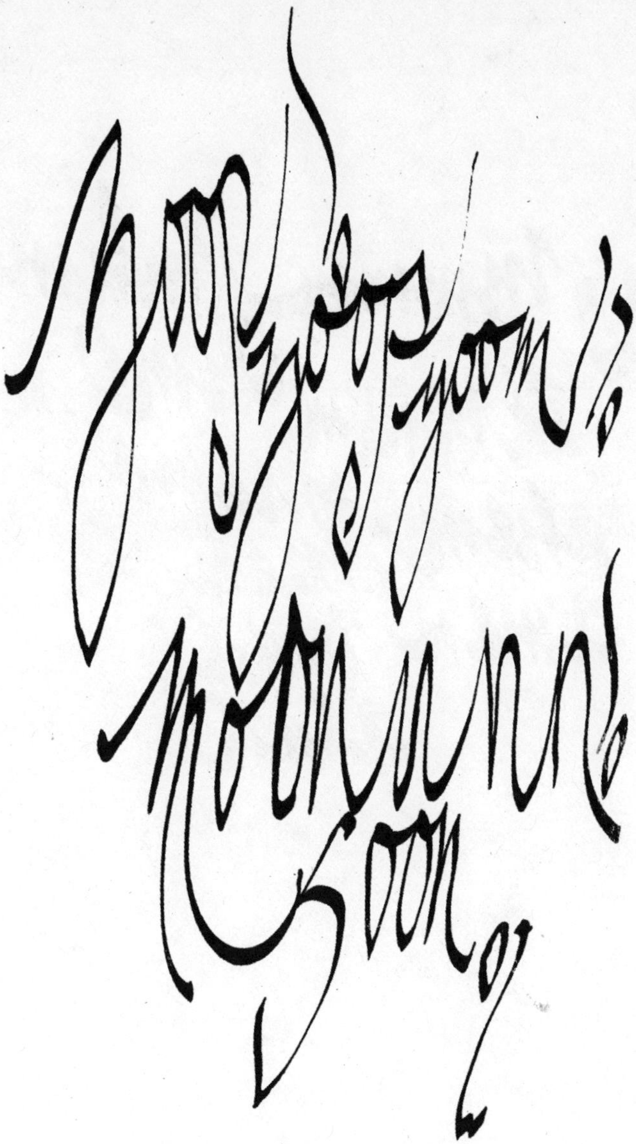

M Mmmm mhmm
Hmmm Ohm
ahem mama
man
amen mad
glad

Another Order

Another Order

Rhythm's gold
Albion's Rose
blooms to calypso
beat

forms an inner
Eye

waves
multiply

preconceive
Deceive
for who can
deduce
Allah's
Master plan

Delights

untold.

Mind
Still
slips
easily
thru
the
clutches
of time

awakening gently intertwine

Morning
Poem

fat
teas
a humming
grass
Wild we
Clover Honey
thick & fine
Dandelion Wine

Children call
run thru time's maze
Sun penetrates gentle haze

Another Order

Horizon

1992

Another Order

Another Order

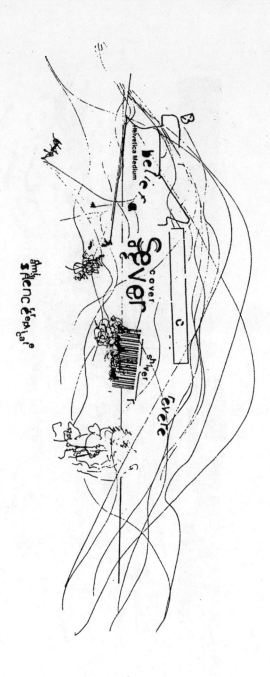

162

Another Order

Brackets & Boundaries
{Concrete & Other Accretions}

2011

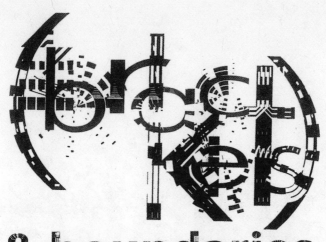

& boundaries

Another Order

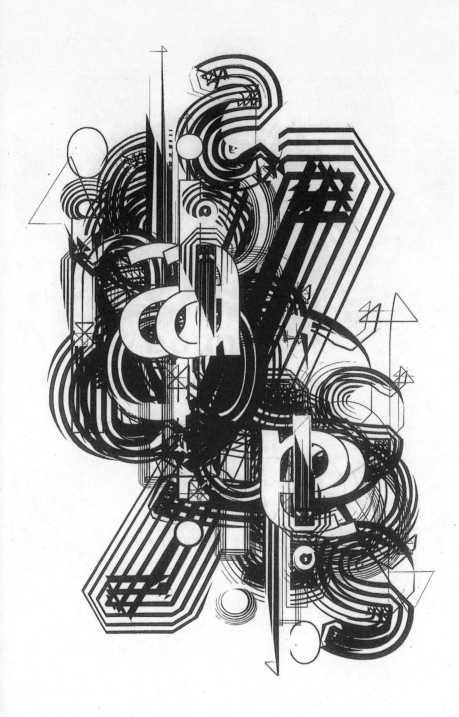

ceramic concrete electronic

phatic/optic   manic/haptic

possiblities of sensations of
perceptual prescience

unearth;
negate/appreciate............................control/rearrange/expand

collisions: elan   a quickening   zealish transports   high-stepping into a
gavotte with its shine still on   fidelity of feeling   willingness of mind
fine mettle   exuberance of intent   movement into softer climes   yet still
a beneficence of breezes ·

ABSTRACTION
&
suspicion
support

tonight: abandoned   empty
open   lucky enough rain washed
silent   with semblance.

Another Order

Another Order

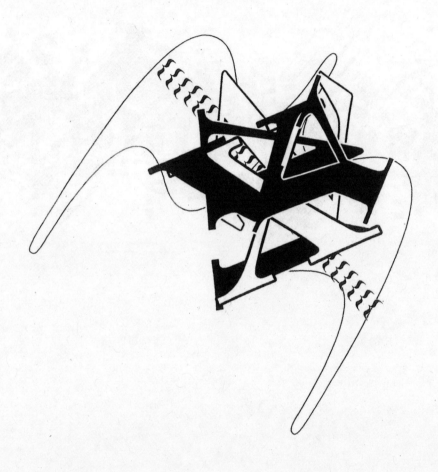

Another Order

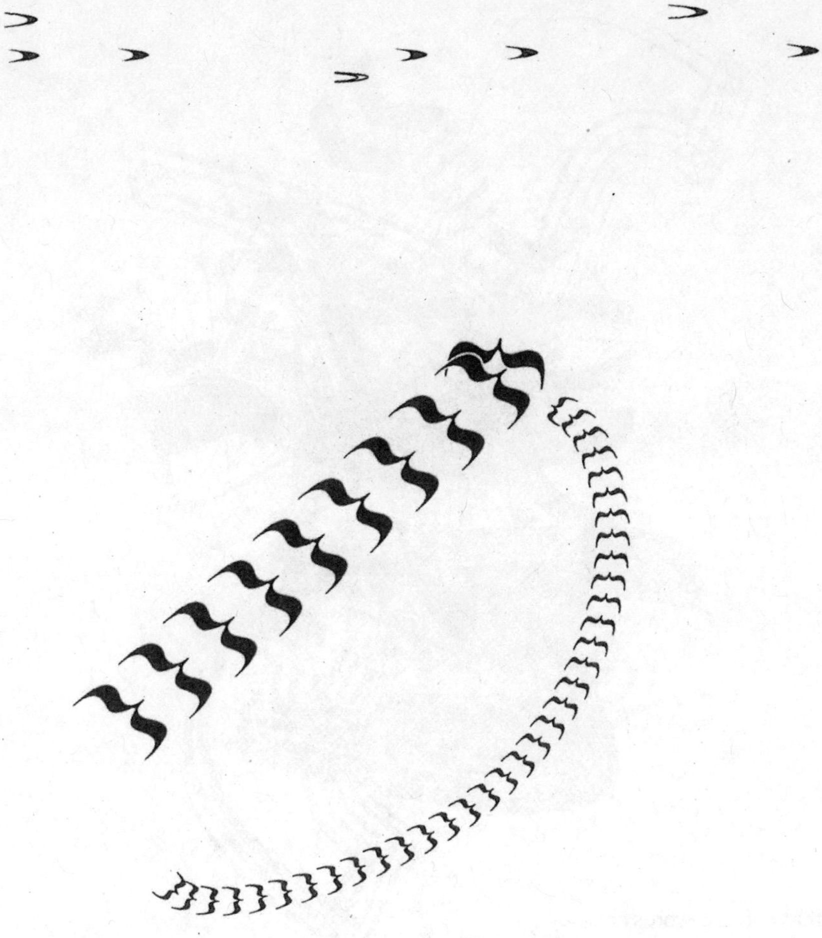

1.

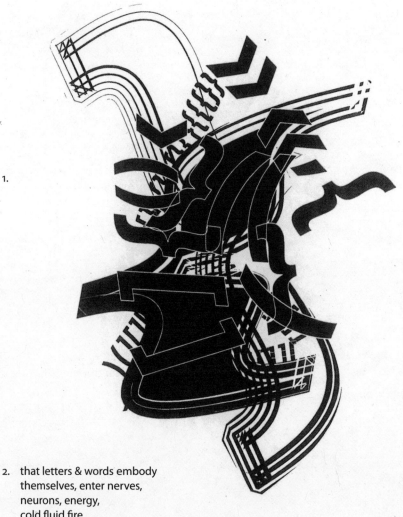

2. that letters & words embody
   themselves, enter nerves,
   neurons, energy,
   cold fluid fire

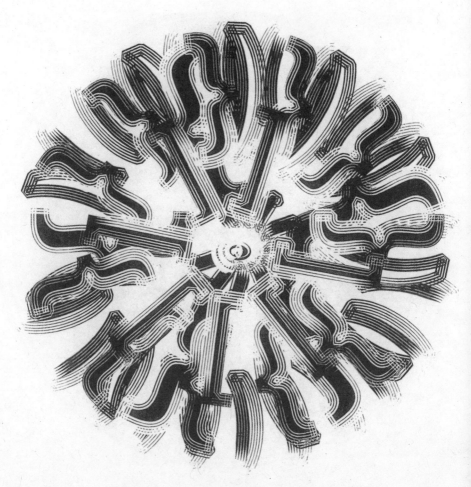

consider the energetics of
mental / social / optic dissonance

Another Order

exploitation expiration – definangling funding
equitable equations – avoiding capital's excess
resetting the wheel of fortune

to break free from this imprisonment
of life's possibilities

dorsal dropped balance enter alone focus
below ground behind back spine
basic erode fall hold on collapse

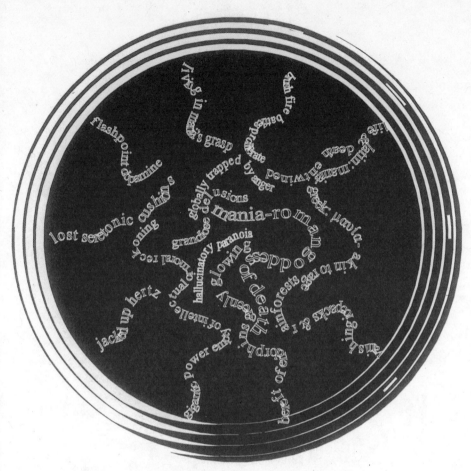

mania – roman goddess of death – latin – mania – greek – akin to rage
flashpoint dopamine – lost seretonic cushions – living in mania's grasp –
jacked-up hertz – bereft of endorphins greenly glowing –
gigantic power empty of moral or intellectual reckoning –
hallucinatory paranoia – grandiose delusions – globally trapped by anger –
brush-fire battles proliferate – vanishing ice caps & rainforests
life & death entwined

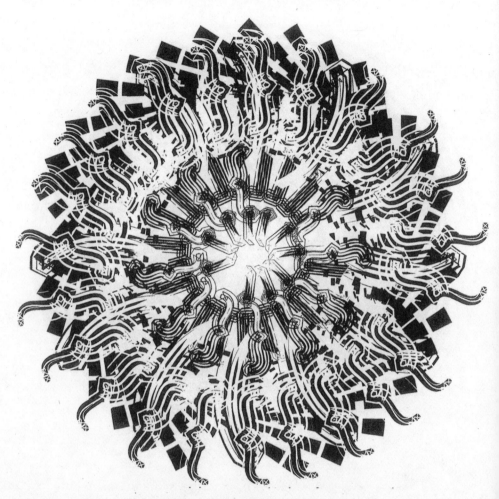

mantua   mandala   wrapped in lace from amsterdam
decoration as abstraction
emotion as survival

the lost vowels:

     in stance ab struse a blute

always a hero in her own eyes

these statistical, memorative, emotional failures

     genetic complexity of the brain

Another Order

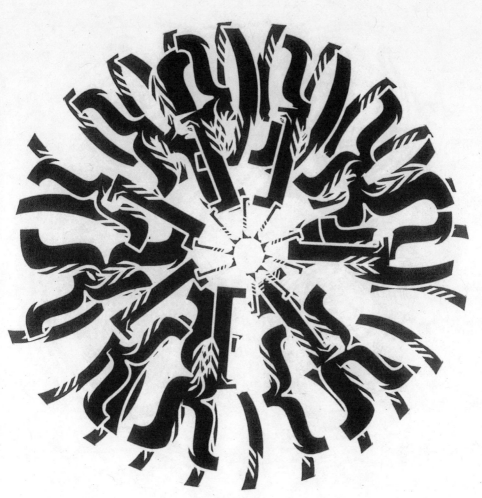

cassandra,
the believers,
& the cynics

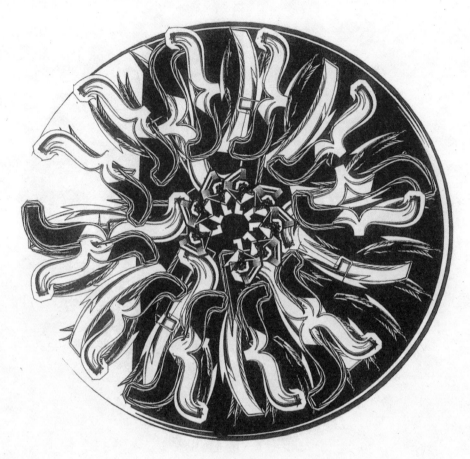

formal explosions
spherical fears
scratch of ideas
whispers of chance

Another Order

– alphabetica – topographic typology –
expending assertion's embrace
gifting sense's caress

state changes affect memory & modelling

lavender, myrrh, sage, balsam fir, grapefruit,
    olive leaf, chaparral, self-heal, lemon balm

heart gone, key likewise
into cracks, behind, done down

Another Order

bracket, n hence v: EF-F ***braguette***, codpiece:
dim of EF-F ***brague***, a mortising, influenced by
EF-F ***bragues***, breeches: L ***brācae***, breeches, pl of
the much less used ***brāca***, adopted from Gaulish,
with r****brāc*** – to encircle, to gird on (e.g., a sword
with its supporting belt).

hinge

                                                                    brackish
                                        ligature
kern   molecular folds

                    tilde

1869 Swinburn Ess & Stud (1878) Byron and Shelley …   *mortise*
I protest against the bracketing of these two names.

                              buttressed

                                                    1869 *Daily News* Jan. 30 only four
          tie{*r*}   times beaten for both prizes, as
                                                           often bracketed
      crochets   contracting

                                                                    *(con)*joined
                    parenthesis

                                              leaving
          [*un*]bound   empty
                          a hold   these dimensions
                          a hole

                    of a {s} *pace*

Lingual – Comments

Concrete poetry, often being about boundaries, invites an examination of boundaries, & in this volume there is also considered a particular form of boundaries, brackets. In the fields of concrete poetry many possibilities abide. The literary plays with & off such areas as those of the literal, the typographic, the personal, & the visual. As in other multidisciplinary & borderland activities, categories & boundaries are often joined, breached, & recombined; thus in this page & in other places in "Brackets & Boundaries" there is unnoted movement between categories.

As a category & an idea, brackets appear to have less scope than boundaries, but to see them on a page is to see a change, a new approach, or to become aware of an aspect of this topic not so often exposed. Typographic brackets are a specific series of boundaries with a particularly interesting set of visual forms. Visual similarities can be seen between typographic & some other forms of brackets.

Brackets & boundaries serve multiple & varied uses, such as those of defining, clarifying, creating backgrounds or foregrounds, or consolidating such attributes as physical substances, support, or power. They sometimes must be stretched or their actions can become severely limited. A large range of categories is being considered together. Brackets are considered in a fairly small proportion of the material. While, contrarily, boundaries often have larger applications, as they do in many aspects of literature or other parts of life.

There are a lot of *A*'s used here. Perhaps the emphasis on *A*'s is a demonstration of a love of beginnings, mornings, the unexpected, a possibility of somewhat unencumbered perceptions &/or actions. Most of these pages are made from complete, partial, or abstracted letters or other forms of typeface.

The interest here may be multiplied by some of the gigantic fields of literature now accessible & may also be multiplied by variety, possibility, change, or chance.

Today, much is explicitly verbalized in or around writing & art which was often deliberately left implicit half a century ago when the intellectual underpinnings of a work were more likely to remain unspoken. & yet neuroscience continues to demonstrate that actions precede thought & language as they appear to act on the brain.

Type which has variable or vanishing boundaries is sometimes used here for examination & description of how permeable many boundaries are & how their appearance & disappearance in our lives often is, or seems to be, beyond our control. Boundaries can be represented by lines & sometimes lines become shapes. Negative & positive space can indicate the interactions of various processes. Inflexible boundaries may then create precarity.

Throughout human history some boundaries have been fluid or entirely mutable, & yet other boundaries have been, & continue to be, militarily maintained by means of surveillance &/or armaments. & those in power continue to attempt to destroy any boundaries but their own.

Phases / Phrases

2019

Phases
Phrases

Judith
Copithorne

My eyes grow dim, my hips more fat, it has happened too fast,
I need another lifetime at least.
Yet possiblities fly from mind embroidering memories of future's pasts.
Colours of dreams cross lightning skies while there opens a world where
reason's farthest reaches presides. There there are dictionaries enumerating,
lazluied power, adrenal imaginations of final dissolutions of extortionate
mercenaries, misers, murderers, and all the enemies of hope.

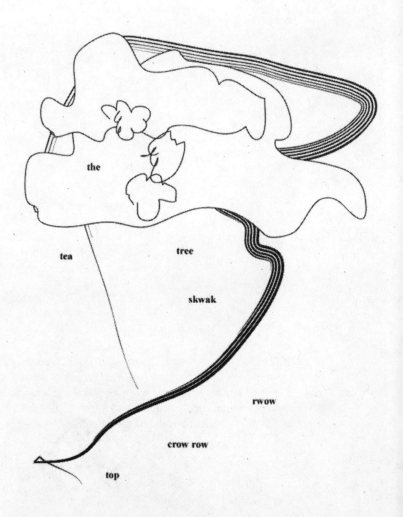

the

tea tree

skwak

rwow

crow row

top

18.3.24 crow

Another Order

19.4.17 short wave

19.3.6 memory

Another Order

19.5.28 return!

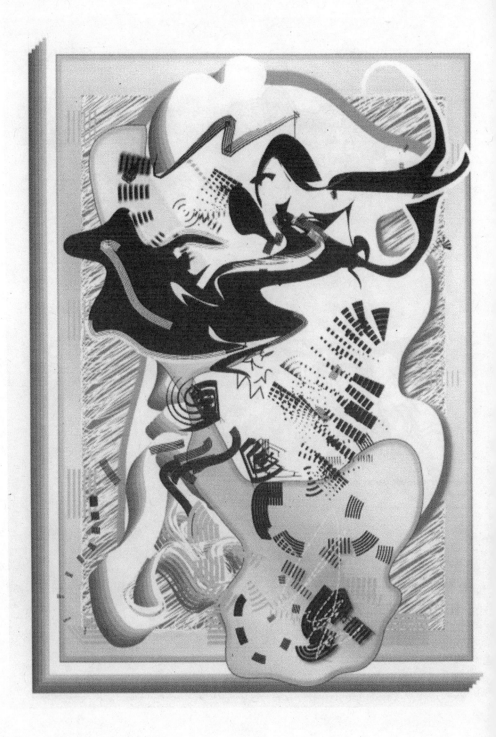

19.7.12 lecture

Another Order

19.11.2 align

19.10.19 I owe Miro

19.11.17 untitled

19.8.15 under

Another Order

splotch

stagger

stock

a cross

smarm

smush

19.5.15 splotch

this universe beyond our imagining what is possible is beyond naming also

Using a brush to make your ideas appear on the page

Discovering methods of mind outside your head

every idea appears on it's own but joins with others before gestation & after it belongs.

19.3.29 idea

19.6.27 paint brush

19.4.27 scape

Another Order

19.6.19 weather

19.5.12 phases

Another Order

Do the mountains walk
back in your sight?

Do trees stalk you at night?

Is your art too odd?
Perhaps you are a
surrealist.

Is your art too
mundane? Perhaps
you are a realist.

Do stalks tree you
even in the light?

Perhaps there are places in the
world or out of it where rules
& names combine. Surrealist, realist
it's all good & mundane & strange,
no reason to complain.

The relativity
of space, of
time, of light, emotions.
Sensation, of ideas, of
experience, of colour.

19.3.20 Perhaps

19.10.24 fall

Another Order

19.4.11 fail safe

19.10.9 greetings

Another Order

ABCDEFGHIJKLMOPORSTU

19.9.30 eyes

19.6.19 wind

Another Order

19.6.25 Sizing

19.2.27 fresh

Another Order

EXplicate

imaginary ideas

Leave the sea of

Extradite

Arise & Recover

Discover the possibility of courage and hope!!!!!

Apprehend & Applaud

tomorrow

An amazing Tell

Color!

Discover pleasure & release

Find the flavor of the future & the heart of further affection.

Dispond

Investigate the Unlikely

Reveal

19.9.10 possible

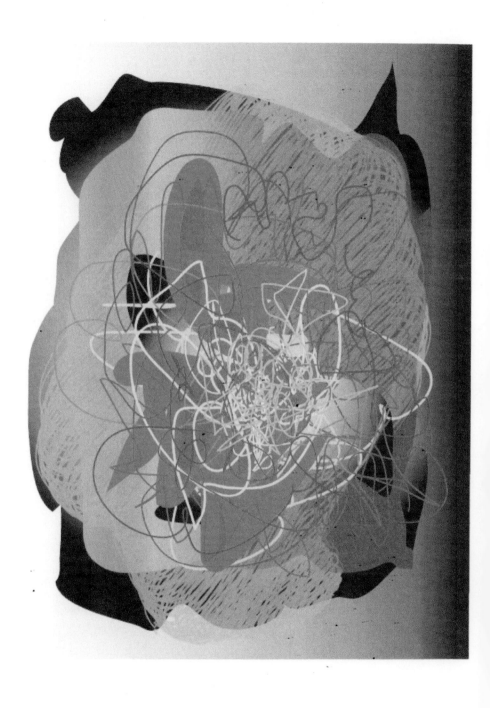

19.6.22 search

Another Order

POETRY

from

Returning

1. honey warms my soul

honey warms my mouth
honey warms my soul
open unto you
your warmth my only goal

sun's in the south
sun's rising high
love's in my mouth
lights up my eye

bright summer day
inside rhythms loud
your song takes me way
high above a cloud

when we trust all this
before force we've tried
when my fears do dismiss
there's unity inside

honey warms my mouth
honey warms my soul
sun's rising in the south
your warmth my only goal

2.   [This lady lived ...]

This lady lived to be ninety-five
        and lived on dates and figs
Little snacks kept her alive
        fit beyond our belief
She only died for the relief

One world for another said her voice sweet
She made every man she happened to meet

Until thirty-three when she took
        a vow of chastity and there
        remained a virgin fair
        loving only in the mystic square
Oh where oh where will you ever see
        a lady as wild as lovely
Most bright most curious 'mongst damsels
Who would undress to the tinkle of bells

3.   Root & Womb

Rooms upon room have my body's soul
To live in and gather whole
Fruit off of our living's tree
So long as my love stays with me

And when he goes my soul knows
No rooms but slips into womb
Then deep to my roots where a hole
She burrows there away from care
Sleeping awhile beneath all guile
Until my love comes again
And life may rise whole and sane

4.   [jelly jelly]

                                    jelly jelly
                          strive goons goons goons
                                            moons
                          strive jelly jelly
                          moons ooms wombs   jelly jelly
                                                push push mush
                                                  mush jump
                          jump jung junk jelly yellow yell hell oh
              scwable

              hooked on such scruff jump down   jump jump volpe
                                      jump jelly jelly
                                      yellow jellow jelly
                                      jelly
                          ah ha belly belly
                                belly-jelly
                              santa claus

5.   Belly Dancer

        She moves in her singular rhythm
        Which underground is everyone's
        We all know her soul for
        Below we meet here too
        In her internal rhythm.
        Her eternal rhythm grows
        All we need
        Her movement knows
        Where our life goes
        And soon we leave our
        Stable places and do believe,
        Forget our grief, delight
        In the love of her body's beat.

6. Mending

With each stitch
Let me hitch up
 my lost
To my reborn
 lives

Reweaving
my roots.

7. And We Gave Name of Flesh to Flame

Within this mesh of flesh drifts
sits sinks into darkness of below
                              our sight the
night of interior flame who we
really are and directs our souls
through lines of gravity.
This flame lives before name and
is heard without word so with
silent life we clothe our
precious eyes in flesh.

8. Returning

A day glides by in its haze
   you gave me those happy days.
I could smell you in my hair
   felt your presence everywhere.
Stranger sing, who were you
   coming up out of the blue?
I came to you because I must
   as I live our life with trust.

As if our centres were one
  of gravity of earth and sun.
Harmony of central beat
  moving us before we meet.
Show the signs of how we loved
  memories live in our blood.

I only know behind it all,
  forgetting this comes the fall,
I am myself all alone.
  I, myself am all I own.

9.   13

13's for moonlight
          and madness my dear
              for the moon's month
                    for leap year
                  so we all have a chance
              and how life will enhance
          our darkest dance
13's for women my dear
              wombs and wonder
          and what's left over
                when you forget your fear
13's for the sea my dear
          and menses and magic
              and movement
      for holidays
      and happiness
          wholeness
          and having your own way
13's for learning your limits
                my dear
          and when it's all over
                remembering to play.

from

Until Now

1971

1.   At First

True, the world needs saving
while, greedy, we do nothing.
How to move the rock, find the joy
inside like honey unlocked from
soft wax to cover mind in warmth.

Seagulls call, starlings chatter
at sparrows, omens of fall.
Small distractions of life show
nothing is worth more than
what you tear yourself apart for.

Whoever you are, wherever we go
however we do, thank you.

2.   Please Yourself Please

It's the clouds covering,
coming down through mind,
which frighten.
Do whatever pleases you, please
when I can't find myself:
sadness and gladness when either can.
You are what you need, your friends are,
soft senses slither down spine.
Now we are together, alone as ever,
all leaves leave trees.
Cold settles down as doubt
feelings in the grey, freeze.
If only you would, could be both
of what you are, without worry.

3.   Evening

Music sometimes says to me,
in its sweetness, there are
so many things which could
have been. Encumbered as I am
with sewing thread and old shoes
how can I live on an island
and walk in morning mist
into rolling breakers of
cold sea? Or know a wilderness
or my own survival alone?
Surrounded by pens without ink
and stiff nerves how will
I respond to this music
which plays my unlived life?

4.   To What End?

You are right
our prettiness appalls, palls
hang in our breast,
indigestion,
emptiness instead of strength.

What to say,
today is safe,
what love exists
belongs to you,
but deeds,
heartfelt movement:
still dreams which hardly live.

Do whatever you please, please
let me please you
greatness lives outside
yet this step is
also not often made:
let me touch you, learn,
and forgive my timidity.

Having lost the track,
doubled back,
ennui overwhelms.
If this all must be destroyed
when do we start and how?

You were dreaming of greatness
and came down into soft mud.
The day sings to itself
and only the wise hear,
they hear everything,
pain, blood, how it is time
for a stronger kind of love.
The air is full of a knowledge
which we see through the smog,
of change, and
how the end must come.

Hot air, cold feet,
smell of harsh gas,
this city suffocates its
not unwilling victims
who can't go back,
and won't come through.
I hear you and your
density of truth
and need the fire too.

5.   Defined

Like chemicals in flux
we charge, change, each other,
the forgotten centre
comes apart.

Bear down, mine rich strata from
the past, rock firm, gem-like,
clear, cold, and hard,
a clarity permeates the mind.

6.   The Always Mystery

And the flooding energy,
wild like the wind today,
when the land turns from soft cocoon
into harsh mountainside,
free beside the bright sea.

Who are we now, the always mystery?
Questions, more than answers
when we: man, woman
body on body: spine moving
are bigger than these words
and these words attain their meaning.

7.   As the Years Turn

Since it all has been given to you
in rain, clear, falling in the alley, why
more and more do you forget to love?
Who is this self you've held so carefully
halfway to winter, the dark coming down,

and only memory of how summer burns.
I wanted, want you, to touch
like wind in spring bushes,
spring is so short in our burden of months.

8.   Sunset

Quiet water
    ocean glow
        in the last
            summer light

truth to tell
tells me
born on mysterious words

growing like one of those trees
wherein dark shadows
        gather
         lacing
          last
            glimmers

        in clearing sky

I write by lamplight
alone
my friends help me
No meaning
    can my mind find

but quiet joy sneaks up
when I forget
to wonder why
I'm alive

Who can be
       that honest
       cut to the bone
       the moment
       and depth of self
revealed
behind shields of society
withdrawn

Who can
    talk
      of desire
        and fear
          and leave
            alone

Unknown
    my changes
       change me

Who
    can
       be?

9.   Tempering

Meanwhile, there are countless stories,
rivers without end, rain plummeting to
the shed roof. Today is felt in shivering
ecstasy, frantic, magic, unknowing.
Dreadnaught trucks roar, images stir
in womb, years pass, love falls nameless
to autumn's track. As we tempered steel,
plunging iridescent blade into oil,
so you drive facts through my heart.

10. Alone

Transmuted finally, you are right,
rain glides out of the sky
its slippery fish ooze, oily
across the street, sidewalk and city,
filter through gas-heated minds.
Is it all pretence, refined beyond
early morning bacon-and-eggs pleasure
of the decadent and healthy?
Conceits of earth turning, bodies
in tune, heart beats in the void,
yes, I know we are all alone.

11. River Runs Round

Turtled in, cat curled, caught in your web,
other, more than world of night coming on,
bound by motorized howls, hair aflame dreams,
inside a head which hears not only with ears.

Crucial as dark rivers of blood, again you
passed through so fast I missed the moving.
Rich dawn light, obscure fruitcake comfort
river runs round, separates friend,
lover, inexorable as mountain or sea.

from

A Light Character

1985

1. ## Siwash Rock

Away, away
across deep level
plains, prairie
snows, or look out
from Siwash Rock.
Away,
looking across and
up, the horizon
changes at last.
The layers shift,
disintegrate,
and the divisions
melt into one.

2. ## [Oh there]

Oh there,
I hear someone calling.
Now let's get this straight
between all of us.
Just who do I hear calling
out in the rain?
When somewhere
a long time back
it was agreed
that there could be
nobody there.

3.   it's a long time

to wait
or to   pause
or
which is
a long time too

4.   The Other Side

I have a green room
with imitation lace
curtains which won't
stay white
they keep being the
colours of things
showing through from
the other side

5.   Red's the Colour

Red's the colour of my love
black is my love's skin
dying's living's closet kin

My heart goes wandering
my mind seems lost
my body's this morning's guest
idea, sensation gather
blood hits skin
the cycle is a month
birth is a year
one month is a turning of
moon and blood

6.   watching

yellow bird
we heard you watching the yellow
bird and we said
she is seeing some colours
singing

7.   Flames

I feel our
our world
on fire
we consume ourselves
in our own passion
destroying our
only dark retreat

Out of
silence
a stranger comes
to soothe
the twisted face
of our suffering
but we cannot
hear him
fire's cracking
obscures his voice
our vision's
twisted by heat

I feel our world
consuming itself
in flames
centred in a

great fireball
gleaming
out in space

8.   Blood and Carnations

Discipline starched clean, hard, white,
warm flow of blood, bright flow of life.
Little dark child,
women lined in rational rows.

A constant rigid regime,
life growing always between
covers of temperature books,
checks of how neat our ward looks.

Charts recording the ways of the moon,
briefly noted, forgotten as soon,
unknowingly following the waves
and rhythms ordering our days.

Deep-red carnations glow dark beside
a night-lit bed where a woman lies,
legs suddenly covered in
her own blood.

Her baby tucked safe in his crib,
she has yet to give the afterbirth,
ripping wall of womb.

The hall is full of flowers,
life coming, going.
Scent of carnations fills the air,
our ward sleeps on under its drug.

9. The Eyes

      The eyes
       studying   one another
swish of evening
       rush-hour traffic
           cold spots of rain
       shoulders
           both of us
hunched against
       winter wind

      The eyes
       studying   one another
       a prolonged
meeting
       strangers   lovers
       friends who never meet

      The eyes
       studying   one another
animal eyes peering
       in the dark bush.

10. The Sun

Burns down
nails me to the rock
Now leap out to sea
deep   weed-filled   cold   holds
salt on me

Sun   broils   burns through
layers of flesh until the mind turns

dark   Eat fire and put it out
Neap tide runs

Sun   the sun   sun beats down
beats down   holds me to the rock
holds me to the rock   burns inside
me   burns without a worry
without a worry   let the mind
do that   after the fact
beats down on me

Eat fire and shimmer in the heat
Here the wind rises around midnight
Right now not a breeze
Night and midday revolve
Crawl up cliff face   swing
high above the tide

11.   **The Rock**

The space becomes more acidic each day
The basement windows are clean
I see you and me and movement of tide
across floor of sea
Sea cabbage and cucumber   starfish
clam oyster and crab
Swim in saltwater   lie on volcanic rock
lava flow from three million years ago
pressed into silicon shard
swift ledges bent and bowed
Swept clean farthest edge of our island
by centuries of wind
lie down above the sea
How can you get comfortable on that rock?

12. **Sunset**

Quiet water
   ocean glow
     in last
        summer light
tell me careful words
   growing like one of those trees
where dark shadows
   gather
     lacing
      last
        glimmers
     in clearing sky

13. **Evening Street**

Strangers pass,
almost silent
in the evening street.
Shapes haloed with delicate hair
Silhouette themselves against
windowpane:
shadows turn in the varied lights
of streetlamps and
cars swishing past
in the wet pavement night.

14. Spring

At the beach

terns and their babies

clear sea

rocks along the beach

and under the water, sea lettuce.

We are all attached.

"The Roshi says, 'If I hit you with a big rock

it's the same as a rose!'"

Everyone on the point together.

Spring

Polarized

Sun and clouds

Dog with red eyes.

On the roof of the ferry.

Mountains all around

tug pulling

mountains white, almost snow

Rain blows in pulp-mill hair.

Beat of engines like a voice.

Ha Ha
Now try climbing out of that hill.

Rosewood ring with amethyst
So long
    the tide comes in.

Sit beside the lead sea
chemical reactions
viscera internal sensations

whitecaps

waves break
salt penetrates
climb the hill
moss bright light green
wind through ponderosa.

Get up, light stove
flame snaps

Arbutus, cedar
grey shoreline

cloud bank mercury rises from
ocean grey-green.

Rain on roof, continuity of night
amplifies tide.

The moment spins us in her
   web of heaven   hell

I dreamed at a door
   smells dragged me in
      whisper in the night
         sleep long into the light.

Salt and sugar
dulse and honey
green stick smells
   find water in the rock.

High-voltage wire
   strike of fire
      a buzz in back of neck
lifting of the hood.

When at world's end two spirals grow
hold me.

15. Sharkaen

We labour to name the disquietude, it may strike
anywhere, does so:
                    we are left / fish on dry lake
bed, flesh burned / sun-dried …
Here the insects keep you moving
discomfort remains the same
we forget from moment to moment
use any solution
still the horsefly bites
away the unquiet gaze.

Gloves, shears, rip aside branches, salal,
huckleberry, juniper, alder, cedar root, maple.
Stars turn in track, logs move, pick up dead
wood for fire, learn the words, try to say
how it at once reveals and hides
the goods we need.

Tied to an infinitely graduated scale
we bend our habits,
children call, horseflies bite,
buzz over cedar log
left squared from shaking,
black raven calls
behind the sun.

Words are everything compared to the trouble of
living. The great earth mother
speaks to me. She says, "You will build
a magnificent house on this very spot
and you will not notice or scratch the bite
just given to you by a gigantic mosquito in the
middle of your forehead."

Suddenly, light flashes off water, through
leaves, flutters on face, voice from canoe calls
up through trees.

Always trying too hard, bumble through, wind
dies, seabird cries, careful with the swede saw.

Down at the bay end they are building a house,
birds sing, alder trees bend in wind,
work never finished, sun goes in.
Spending our lives on nothing ...
if this could be sorted into categories
we would know
where the money goes /
what we have done wrong ...
Someone passes on the path above, pulls grass,
tide creeps up / licks around feet,
the boat from town not yet appeared.

Whistle, hammer in the garden, jet overhead, city
again, pick up parsley, lettuce, books, head
uphill ... how to move / round cars.

16.   A World Being Made

Perched, here, on the stool, while out on
the street people move, busy towards noon,
having taken care
of too many particulars,
now there is time.
The memory clings like smell
and the city glows below
beautiful and cold as the sea.

I know what I must say,
I have taken leave,
gone out to find you or something.
People pass, discrete entities in the
clear morning breeze, maple leaves
leave branches.

17.   Jericho Beach

Down to Jericho, pick up coffee ... Not bad, I tell the man ...
he beams ... It's good a ya to say that (Scottish brogue).
Gather up bag, walk across sand, right up to great barbed-
wire fence, rusty holes patched with boulders. I've lost it. Go
to the first big boulder, move up, second hole blocked. There
it is, the third hole ... No, it's blocked with old, corrugated
metal, rusty spikes, chewed up, bashed-about car door. They
were serious. Stop. Put up hair ...

Do you want to go through? ... Faded T-shirt, a smelt
fisherman ... I'll let you through ... Just an old man put up
that sign ... and then I blocked that second fence off, to keep
those other guys out of my net ...

No, I'll get through ... down to low water ... that other hole
is still open ... comes up behind me as I crawl through the
wet sand, sliding under knees, water lapping, watch the rusty-
metal jagged ends, sunlight on rocks, look across smooth tidal
flats ...

Water cold, clean, flashes past / off arms / salt, clear / into
nose, arms cutting, body moving / no thought.

No fish here like there used to be ... ten years ago I made nine thousand dollars and then went log salvaging ... used to be you couldn't buy those nets ... made my own ... this year they sold seven thousand of them at the Army & Navy ...

Swim again / salt water cures.

He scrutinizes. Can't swim you know. How many stories a week do you write? Not many ... we sit on the beach. Well, you're busy, won't disturb you ... clinker disappears around pier, tall grass shines in sunlight, water laps white corks.

Rena appears, fisherman follows, lugs a two-four ... they drink beer.

A scuffle, he's following her ... You're too damn smart ... You think I won't pinch your ass? ... Get away you stupid ... He looks like he might hit her with the oar, they move behind the logs, he jams the oar locks, no it's her, she starts out in his clinker ... he, in the long grass, pees.

Now a fire / she lights matches / crams torn branch down smelt throat / blood seeps / thick, coagulates around wood / eyes bulge / flames crackle / oily smoke, sparks, ash blown by winds / fish browns, skin puckers, cook, bake, meat seared, civilized, hands removed from near flame, eggs removed, thrown back to blaze.

He grabs her ... go away! He gathers bottles, leaves.

We cover the fire with sand and leave.

18.   Market

The store around the corner has gone, just
went by yesterday and there it was, less
fruit than before but still there and now today
it's gone with only the cases to remind you
of it, actually it's not much different than it
was before, just a little barer really, some
of the colour gone, and the old man with the
blue open-worked skullcap his wife crocheted
for him, and his big bony wife who smiled her
gold-toothed smile at you each time you came in ...
Gradual, it was that change in the quantity and
each thing got older, sat on the shelf for
longer each time ... Washing soda is something
hard to get and they carried that and bok
choy, washing soda was the only thing I bought
there recently as a matter of fact.

19.   [Paper flowers, Italian wax matches ...]

Paper flowers, Italian wax matches in a little delicate box
covered on one side with a yellowed picture of Lake Garda –
a pink-walled house, red-tile roofed, backed by cypress trees
and pink clouds against lilac hills on a turquoise, blue, and
liquid-green lake. On the other side, the Dolomites rise in
strange, badlands formations behind a little, yellow peasant
house, thick, rusty-red against a bright, blue-and-green sky.

20. [flower]

> flower
> house
> roll dog happy
> eating up the leftover
> food, filling up the
> old books, covering
> up the forgotten

21. Dream

> Pictures glitter,
> we run through enormous sewers
> like those in Hong Kong.
>
> They were effete, even to their harems
> perfect grace like red temples carved
> in stone. Great slabs, pale, rosy
> gashes in the desert.
>
> Or the city made out of granite, lit with
> gold light.
>
> Clear layers, image cortex,
> cerebrum.

22. A Light Character

It's
to give back
    kindness,
    strangers, gifts
If kids see pleasure they are pleased
A white horse with wings
children's songs

A sequence required
    no mistakes. It's too late to stop. The day
is late. Power as in skill etc. old saws.

The typing book says:
If you keep your back straight and your feet
on the ground you will succeed.

Death, she looks like.
A fool rattles his bones.
A mind requires answers.

Reading my mind home from the marina
Regionalism, desire.
Necessity stylized utterance

       A true romance.
Meanwhile time passes, some people, those people
They all know
       the yellow, canary colour showed
       a light character

He knew how to tell a real story.
His lips were full of a story she wanted to
be in. She touched his lips but the story
eluded her. She didn't want to steal but

she wanted to open what was in him.

23. After Frida Kahlo's Painting
My Nurse and I

Blood flows into ocean
moon falls into sea
the heat, a turbine, spits
    electrical charges.
Lungs, a transformer, stepped down
    incalculable power from
    giant pylons to terrible
steel poles pinning Frida Kahlo,
piercing pelvis and spine.
Its cables striking
seconds after the
collision, steel on steel of
the lumbering bus in
the city.

Moon mother
watch over your child
heavy with image,
constant pain, broken
into new life. Alive in
jungle, leaf, tendril,
weird geometry, open
nipple spits milk.

24. Empty

He didn't have to explain,
maybe that's poetic.
It's supposed to be that way,
the engine and the bedpan.
Yeuk!
A dirty choice is clean,
basic instincts
but I couldn't (leave it alone).
Cable cars
a peony
death
pain
continuity.

25. Recipe for Acidophilus

Get out recipe for acidophilus
wash dishes to clear space
go to store to buy milk
look up boiling point of water
play with cat
have a nap
wash out dishes and pan
heat milk
answer door
reheat milk
mix culture
place over pilot light
talk to cat
go next door for a chat
return
leave pan on pilot light all night
it works fine.

26.   [No time to get back ...]

No time to get back to machinery or the plum trees
the men just pruned this morning.
The keys clack. The next stanza, she says! Imagine writing
with mind and hand so close they coincide.

This is a charm,
it will make me strong, the choices will not be difficult,
the rules line themselves up on the wet side of the fence.
It won't be long before the continental drift of my inertia
stops us altogether and a new method is assumed, such as
prayers wrapped in fish skin in the belly of thought.

Sunlight, which is like your voice which is saying,
your voice is like water running.
What a nice thing to say. How did you think that up?
He's so charming.

27.   1915

My mother didn't want to go to church
Finally she told the minister that he was
          lying about God.
My grandpa said she shouldn't
          say such things but
wouldn't tell her if he agreed about God.

He and Grandma called each other Lovie.
Grandma knitted beautiful sweaters
and when she was dying she
told my mother she was not afraid
for she knew she would meet
Grandpa after she died.

28. [Vegetables in the pot ...]

Vegetables in the pot, pot on the stove. Outside the snow
is still, white, the shadows are blue. It is overcast and
still snowing. The loss of words fades. The fire under the
mountain reaches heaven, the japonica blooms. Those
mistakes were a source of new satisfactions. A raven shines in
the snowy breeze, he just flew away. The snowflakes twist and
turn in the white-and-grey sky. The raven twists and turns in
the snowy sky ... The raven was sitting on the telephone wire
which is blue-black and topped with a rim of white snow.

29. [I can see the ridge ...]

I can see the ridge in front of one section and the slightly
darker area behind it that acts as an outline. The variation
in colour ranges from brownish-green to dark green-blue.
There are brown-green areas where the sun is hitting cleared
sections or burned sections or rocks covered with a light
ground cover, then there are the light-green sections which
are the evergreens and shrubs where the sun hits them and
the dark blue-green is the usual mountain colour where the
late afternoon rays are not hitting and the trees are shading
one another.

30. Sunday Morning

The fireweed is in bloom against the fence, three girls pass in shorts and sun tops and the street is silent again. There is a red strip running through the bottom-quarter line of the view through my window. On the strip, through the trees and wires there is the white word SERVICE. Another person appears in a yellow T-shirt against the blue of the Smithrite container; he passes along the street bouncing the pack on his back into a comfortable position. The little plum tree has nice green leafy foliage. Two more people walk by, the morning glories climb the fence, you know that if you stay here long enough the birds will fly up as they just did. Now someone is taking a picture, now he and the person he is photographing are out of the picture, the Chinese man, he lives down the block, just walked by wearing his old country-style clothing.

A green car, another car passes, the two children are playing so nicely with a cardboard plane, or more likely balsa wood. Now they have gone behind the tree, I think one was an adult. The child laughs, the plane whisks across the parking lot, flying beautifully this time on the wind. It is an adult crossing the lot with him, maybe it is his mother or sister, she is definitely shorter than the large man who crossed a minute ago. The plane whisks around a few more times, two more.

Girls pass. There seem to be only young people around today. The plane now flies beautifully when the girl flies it. Two people are watching from above, a woman in a pink robe and another woman. The pink is a wonderful pale pink. The plane just flew into their third-story balcony door, you can hear them laughing … the plane flies as fast as those birds flying about so fast you can hardly see them. A couple of bald-headed men pass. Now everyone has gone. The sky is blue, the mountain is blue, the cars pass fast, the streetlights shine from the sunlight bouncing off their metal casing.

31.   [I know the exact date]

I know the exact date
because it is necessary
for my job.
My job
is necessary
so I can
drink a beer when
I come home and
sit down and write,
hopefully.

32.   [Continual decisions ...]

Continual decisions which want to be heard.
The radio mutters away in the kitchen.
"Don't waste any paper." "Don't blunt that
felt-tipped pen." "After all, it's Friday night."
A happy cliché.

33. [He keeps talking ...]

He keeps talking about mortality
he seems to relish it.
The skull burned in the
flames, turned black
and to ashes and the
ashes blew away
into the cold, blue
sky. The voice
keeps telling us that
life is without continuity,
that the dead man has
now reached new realms
and that the circle
turns continuously.

34. [Kuan-Contemplation, View]

1. Kuan-Contemplation, View

I paste little notes on my wall
I try to remember

Images of flowers in a hot summer breeze
        in a country graveyard
            or arboretum
scented lilies and the perfume
        of stocks and wallflowers
and dry summer grasses

2.

The I Ching tells me I have lost my faithful
helper through my rude actions.

3.

I need to write this so you will understand.
I live on a hill. The wind blows. Lightning strikes.
Clouds condense. Airplanes fly overhead.

4. Reunion

I said to Peggy, try writing every
day, it'll be good.
Peggy said, it might be good and
it will be obtuse.

Barb said she read poetry when she
was very open to things and then it
made her more aware of her own feelings.

35. Affirmative Poem

What we want are words
intelligent words
words that mean something
means that mean something
        mean life and fire and danger
        then the quiet after the danger
            has gone

Words that cause pleasure
        and make us question
we will use words that clarify
        and satisfy and the words
will show us things

We have words to enlighten
        and to enlarge

Songs will rush out of our mouths
We will destroy ignorance with words
We will speak words
        and our words will make forms
I will speak happy words
        and strong words
            words of affirmation
            and words that make sense
            that help us understand
Beautiful pictures will come
        out of our mouths
Words will rush to us
        like a river of stars
The form will form us and formed
        we will form

36.   Wednesday Morning

The postman is walking across the street. J.C. just
walked by and a woman in a grey velvet coat. The
haze has gathered around the mountains. Dark haze,
it could be snow. The street is empty and the light is
warm, touchable. Alex crosses the street in his green
jacket. Things speed up, steady. Cars pass, a trolley-
bus aerial runs along wires another street over.

Crows caw behind the building and there is one in
front, at the top of the pole. The street is quiet now –
or the view is – a MacLure's taxi passes, the crow calls
again, the clouds almost totally cover the mountains,
a woman passes with dry cleaning in her arms, her
hair up on top of her head, the crow has gone. A man
in racing gear passes on a bicycle, another trolley
aerial floats beyond the laundromat sign. Someone
in a black duffle coat turns the corner, the nearest
building is a soft cream colour and its tone rapidly
fluctuates as the light does. The sky gets higher
behind the building. To the north a white seaplane
flies, the clouds on the mountains are still dark. The
plane disappears. There are candy-striped awnings on
the two-storied white building, a man loads a wicker
hamper into his car. Trucks and cars pass.

37. Emblem

This morning
you were silver fire
you gave me energy
and pulled the world
together

Now it's fading
but I want
to make
an emblem
for myself

38. [I want you ...]

I want you to touch my breasts. I want to lick
you. I want you inside me, it feels like
the morning dew. I feel soft and rested and
cool and refreshed. It makes me feel whole
and new. The burning stops and I'm open to you.

39. The Yellow River

There is a yellow river in my dreams
which flows through me and carries
peace with it ... no more stale milk
for little babies, no
more refusing assistance to old people,
no more atomic energy, no more
nuclear warheads, no more hate

The river is death and eats us up until
we become eternity ... it is very clear,

the rhythm is there in its rolling, huge
delicate waves, the whirlpools boil
over in clear, golden eddies giving us
pleasure and power and insight,
inspiration and strength, swallowing
us in its inundations

The river gives us names and strength, we
stop the depression and replenish the empty
reservoirs, we give images to everyone
which they love and the citizens
rise up and stop the war
We find words that
make people understand
and they are no longer afraid

40. Almost Spring

This is a collage – close tonal gradations,
    soft greys, magic patterns, secret.
The plum tree is in bloom again.
        Typical responses occur, I keep my mouth shut,
fill in papers all day so as to have something to say.

There is a beautiful spring light. It's warm. The light
fades. That's the bright sun going down, it has eluded
clouds all day.

    (Rose's pearls were fastened with diamond studs.)

    My bright friends were clearly there yet you could
see through them at the same time.
                        (I can barely remember
the transparent curtains in my green room.)

The story we listened to had anecdotes and wild narrative form. He told wonderful stories. They consumed themselves in his voice and a few memories remained.

People vanish leaving emptiness in the day.
The image changes itself.
It's a beautiful spring night.

They loved each other and by the time I looked they seemed old. Lots of things happened. The backyards stretched out forever. I remember them first as perfect gardens. I remember trying to use those words. I don't remember sequences. The children were wild or dazed. It doesn't turn out the way you expect.

The book said people use divination to see what is apparent, which they cannot see because of their confused state.

I want to tell you, "Like me because I like you."

I want you to make more, will it into emptiness except for me and you.

The forsythia blooms and the daffodils. Out in the valley, at Bradner, the fields of spring flowers, Dutch tulips and more daffodils open up.

PROSE
AND
OCCASIONAL
WORK

from

Heart's Tide

1972

JANUARY 22 (FULL MOON)

Told Elli the story about Bartolome last night. She said it reminded her of a story her grandmother told her, of a dybbuk. Maybe I can at last write it down. It seems a steady enough time right now, living alone, meditating a lot, working hard. Maybe at this point the lack of distractions will turn around and show a positive side, a space from within which I can look back, see where I've been, where I'm going.

Where to start? Try to get to the guts if I can. The bus was waiting to pull out, I sat hoarding both seats. A face jumped out of the crowd of loading passengers. A face darker than some. Heavy features, sculptured. Beyond all the specific details, something which aroused my curiosity.

FEBRUARY 8

The sea is large and lonely. Too bad to be a woman looking for a man who disappears. Ducks and terns swim round the rocks before me. A flight of swallows across the fog, sun comes through, lighting the beach water rush fog, blanket, cuts roar of city, smell of salt air fills lungs.

FEBRUARY 18

Greg came by. He seems kind. I must be mad, he has a wife and son.

FEBRUARY 19

Talked to Matilda about Greg. Greg described Matty as looking like oatcakes and very healthy and wholesome. She laughs and smiles, delightfully, infectiously, so convincingly that no one realizes when she is going to crack up. She is blond and she giggles, will play the clown.

Make it all work, make it all dance and sing, what is their world for if not to enjoy. Love is a funny thing which eludes those who search for it.

Matty sees it when it comes and lets it go again. Once she told me that all the time she was growing up her mother competed with her for men who were more the age of Matty than they were of Leah. Now Matty won't compete, rules out jealousy completely. She went out today, with her father. He is a handsome man of the same kind of blond beauty which belongs to Matty. When he came he brought us four gorgeous roses, two fuchsia pinks, one crimson, one a huge white bud. They sit there now on the table in my Arabian brass jar. His gestures are really almost perfect, he has that continental consciousness of grace which values beauty almost to the same degree as did the hippies.

The exclusivity of love is perhaps its most curious face. It's a bond we only feel at certain times and in particular places. How eros joins us only to certain people and with them the bonds are very vital and hard to displace.

Image: black typewriter, silver-lined black keys. All along I have tried to keep writing out of this. To limit and train the scope of the characters but it is no longer satisfactory. Grey kitten on the gold stole, curled up and purring, at last willing to be friendly.

FEBRUARY 24

Yesterday Greg came and we made love. He hasn't called today. The void. Always ending up looking at yourself.

MARCH 2

Everyone must have a vision. Some are smaller than others. Carry less weight. Centre less gravity. But nonetheless profound. Now what was he talking about? All I could hear was my breath. Why all this trouble to define the light? "Love is a plastic form of light."

We are all haunted by our own masks.

And then we are left alone again. Rainbow image. So then, too, some things remain unknown. Five o'clock and it is too late to see you now. I'm sad at having missed you but the conditions were too hard. Eros, the love that burns. How much loving can you do in so little time?

MARCH 21 (SPRING EQUINOX)

Chemical reactions. The 108 disturbing passions. A chain of breath. Hold me tight. Catch me when I come, come to me. If you are moving on, let me know.

Remembering Bill. Wouldn't make love with him that night and he was found dead the next morning.

This path keeps leading to fire. A fire across the street last night. Learn to burn gracefully. Lace in the flames. Rippling up the walls. Liquid fingers of light. Three houses within our neighbourhood burned last week, sounds like shells exploding, bursting glass.

Greg, you took me, but my body's been left behind.

MAY 5 (NEW MOON)

Beach today. When I write I show myself to be different than I expect. The discovery is continuous although not always pleasant. Greg came yesterday. And the thought of children comes and goes. The myths that obscure the blunt reality. "You're heavy," he says. Like a junky. It really hurts when he says these things. Yet they are true. Internal monologue transformed by romantic genius into magic, myth, which gives us little hint of the real situation. To return to where, to when? Here, where I sit, I say I won't go to him again. He must come to me after those things he said. Yet I want him. I don't know why. I should have left it all alone. Why can't you let it go?

"Gate, gate, pāragate, pārasaṃgate, bodhi svāha."

"Gone, gone, gone beyond, gone altogether beyond, all hail." Should have passed on that first day he was on the beach. I was superbly confident. One of the great days of my life. Things had flowed out of themselves all day long. At noon I reached the top of the hill, supposed to be shopping, had a schedule all worked out. Then I saw the sea, it seized me. The same as today, all blue and saltfull. So I rushed down the hill and trudged along the beach. Smiled at each person I passed. Walking straight, suddenly I saw him, we were walking in each other's path. So I kept on going, came right up to him. We exchanged greetings and passed on. The light of the sea came flooding in on me.

Full of delight in the sunny summer morning came Hanna at five years old. Dressed in her distant aunt's long-ago party clothes. Old Cuban-heeled shoes, a hat which seemed rimmed as wide as a picture window on her small head. Trailing along behind her the skirt of somebody's sometime, a long-ago summer rayon, flowery-printed dress falling limply.

"Now I am a woman of the world. I can go as my mother does. I can walk up the street to adventure freely."

She came to the top of her block where, on one hand, the road led up the hill to streetcar lines and shops and on her other hand stretched down the steep hill to the beach. Beyond that lay the whitecapped bay, the outer harbour of Burrard Inlet, where far out on the water were floating bells, fishing boats, barges, and tankers.

The sunlight moved over the restless sea leaping in white-crested waves. An ever-changing arm of the illimitable ocean caught momentarily and constantly in this inlet.

A shimmering and a sheen leapt up from every spray of water the sun's rays touched. Eyes, once they had glanced at the deep-blue bay, were caught in a glow of solar refraction. All the harbour air seemed filled with a white-gold sheen.

Surely, there's no harm in going to that ocean beauty! But she knew she should not think of travelling so far from home. One part of her now was a grown lady dressed in high heels and a picture hat. This lady could go anywhere adventure and beauty lured her, she had only to choose between the civilized adventures up the hill or the beauty of ocean below. Still there was another part of her held deeper within where she now almost heard her mother's voice telling her she was just a child, she would hurt herself, she couldn't walk so far anyway, how would she get back, her parents even now would be worrying about her. This deeper voice which she tried now to calm would be with her even when she was a grown woman, returning too soon to a place where there was certainly no one waiting.

Her black dog was in ecstasy at having reached the top of the hill, he ran here and there up the road, into the bushes, across the street up a back alley, pissed on a garbage can, rooted in the hydrangeas, smelled the compost heaps and all the clothesline poles. Then he ran back down the alley, down the road to the ocean. He turned, wiggling all over in anticipation, watching her to see where she'd go next.

She just stood watching him and the day, feeling the adventure within. The excitement of her journey grew in her, slowly stilling those questioning, conflicting voices.

Black dog Nebuchadnezzar: When he was a small puppy named this because her father said, "He ate grass."

Nebby, for short, was her companion, he ran free always, was like a guide to adventure.

If her needs within were joined to an exterior symbol, through this material evidence her action was fortified.

"Where are you going, Nebby?" she called. Nebby ran on. "Nebby, Nebby, come back," her black dog could not desert her.

He turned, to entice her on to search, or desiring to answer her voice yet unwilling to return tamely home so soon. She walked towards him, as well as she could, in her Cuban-heeled shoes and trailing dress, all of which lent her the necessary dignity for the journey yet constantly threatened to trip her.

Farther down the hill they went. She, who first wished to catch her dog to return home, soon was following her black animal guide. Entranced by the morning shadows of leafy poplar trees, treading on a sidewalk covered with green, summer-sweet-smelling grass cuttings and pungent pine needles. In the gardens beside the road grew huge dahlias, rich-smelling roses full of humming bees, the manure of these gardens, careful gardeners ringed the fertile air. Then there was the wild, rainforest, deserted stretch of vacant lots. Tangles of morning glories, wild thorny blackberry vines, coral salmonberry flowers, golden furry dandelions which when you picked them left their milky gluey juices covering your hands.

Time was long gone.

She followed Nebuchadnezzar down a trail in a land of light, all only sunlight, warming, leaf-shaded, green glowing.

Suddenly they were at a huge highway, a wide wide road. Just beyond she could see the sea. The high hill behind her stretched high high, too many miles away was her home. Cars hurtled by. Nebby could lead this far, faith, see the sea, see the light. The sunlight became sea light filling her eyes.

Nebby rushed into the traffic and out again, cocky, excited, not wishing to leave her yet wanting to get to the ocean. She lifted her trailing skirt firmly in her left hand, placing her right hand on her head to hold her hat close from the wind of the cars swiftly rushing past. Clenching her toes in her clattering ladies' shoes, she started to walk only watching Nebby and the shimmering water beyond. If traffic was screeching to a halt on either side of her passage she never heard or knew.

Now beneath the great virgin trees still standing at the beach edge she was treading on firmly packed sand. Finally she stood beside the ocean. The wind blew from the west, from far away out in the vast Pacific, straight into her face. Her hat blew off, her shoes were filled with sand. She bent and buried her face in the ocean. Cold cold, life water, slither of seaweed, elemental, first smell of salt. First smells of shellfish, barnacles, and clams, and of all the dying which is constantly coming to the sea to be transmuted into new growths.

Seagulls dipped and rose overhead, out to sea and back again, in full wild curves on mysterious invisible wind currents. Their strange, rusty cries seemed inseparable from the smell of salt. The water, golden where sunlight shimmered on it, was so cold and silver-green beneath that it burned her feet. The train of her hanging rayon dress was soaked and icy cold, the sand felt harsh to her cold-burned feet.

Gathering her costume, she moved inland to the sheltering, sun-dried upper beach. Here between tall evergreen trees of a once-silent forest and the edge of the never-tamed ocean, lay a strip of soft loosely packed glistening white dry sand. Sand full of tiny pieces of dried ocean life, slices of shells of dead-and-gone shell creatures, partial bones of long-ago-eaten fish, fragments of seaweed, tiny pieces of coral, salt all crystallized, sparkling beside every grain of sand. Sand fleas leaped. Huge salt-and-barnacle-encrusted logs, washed onto shore in storms, from logging booms, lay piled at intervals.

She sat in the lee of one of these piles of logs for a while, smelling their accumulated tales of their long travels from forests hundreds of miles up the coast. She watched Nebby run in and out of the incoming tide licked by the sea foam, barking at seagulls, snuffing, digging with his nose for clams. The sun warmed her here, dazzling her with its glow until all her fears disappeared. She was too old from her adventures to build a sandcastle. Once she was warmed she moved on up the beach with her black dog.

Beyond her to the east, the arm of the inlet reached past this outer harbour, around past many white beaches, a heavy green forest part, and a high-arched bridge span into Vancouver's centre and inner harbour. Walking along the warm beach to the east, towards the morning sun, she could see the brightly sunlit silvered towers of downtown.

Grownups appeared from the trees to the side and ahead of her walking west. Passing towards this group she walked proudly, an equal, at first wondering if they noticed this lady she was. Then she immediately forgot them as she walked alone towards the eastern sun.

The grownups noticed her and a woman who carried her body watchfully, with a worried manner, detached herself from the group running towards Hanna, arms outstretched, calling Hanna's name in a wild clear voice. Then Hanna's mother was beside her distraught, gesturing, questioning.

Hanna could find no way to tell her mother of the sun glow and sea life she felt moving all around them.

MAY 6

Losing myself again. The day is beautiful and so are you. Sitting on the far end of the rickety wharf of the commercial marina under the Burrard Street Bridge. The sound of the cars high up crossing the huge cement edifice almost harmonizes with the sound of the water. Meditate on the huge bridge pillars, on ocean water rushing past in the channel, on the vagaries of love. Can things be forced if they are not ready to come? When is a love affair not one? Almost always today, maybe. Oh women pretending innocence. "They only die for love in the movies," Don said the other night and we all giggled helplessly. It's all right now to sound so tough, but who does when they are really left alone? Still a little bit of tough hide goes a long way to save some useful talent. Maybe someday we can have both.

When I met Greg we were in two separate worlds and we still are. Some of us live hopelessly in our own minds. Have no way of getting out it seems. Maybe he helped me get out for which I can only thank the Gods. Women are poor weak creatures, throw themselves away helplessly. Men do too. Find me a balance: something we're all facing. Stories are often too close to home. How we hate to reveal ourselves. Maybe I can't write this but I'll try.

He has a terrific presence. "Aries people have," he said when I mentioned that. A physical presence, which draws an immediate response from me. A madman I might say. But not that crazy really only extremely full of life, coming and going constantly. Power is probably his ruling sign although he wants more than that.

A square man built like a Mayan sculpture, or one of the Tantric demons.

Spring is the most beautiful time of year here, the possibilities present themselves again anew. When I was young, we'd ride our bicycles out along Marine Drive to Spanish Banks and climb the great clay cliffs and carve our initials in the banks, sometimes we'd write the name of our current love. We'd find those great furry caterpillars, orange-and-black tiger-striped, play with them for hours, then bring them home and create a world for them in a shoebox. Pile the box first with soil then with moss and plant ferns and tiny bushes, with a jar lid full of water disguised as a pond in one corner of the box. A sort of Rousseau jungle and just as unreal for soon the soft, almost blind, kitten-like creatures would fold themselves into cocoons and never come out again. Once I kept the cocoons all winter in my precious box but the caterpillars never hatched into butterflies or moths.

Later, Spanish Banks was a place for going with a boy in his own or his father's car. You'd sit in the car and make awkward talk, sometimes exchange tentative kisses.

This spring, living alone again and at last beginning to relish the freedom and joy it can bring, I wander out to Spanish Banks again and see that almost supernatural light at sunset. The city from there seems like a fairyland, and the mountains glow, pure blue silhouettes in the last rays of the sun. The banks of mountain become a slightly lighter blue in careful, hard-edge order as they recede from view, eventually becoming merged with the hazy horizon and sky's pale blue.

Went out to the mudflats today. Driving, out through town. Hare Krishna temple corner. Concrete images. Grey long, blocks long, building, many windows. Sky getting darker, Princeton Hotel, car behind me, turn into Wall Street, along one row before the industrial waterfront. Looked up the charioteer yesterday at Marsha's and it signified the highway with no end, the light which binds us in from the darkness which is brightness which is too great for us to see with naked eyes. Platonic instead of Aristotelian or archaic. Empirically the cyclical theory of history is a fraud. Unfortunately, it still keeps coming up.

How not to disturb the changes, keep on the subject. Wall Street has some horrible apartment buildings. Has some old houses of various shapes, old shacks with multicurved porches. Rococo latticework, salt-air inlet. Drive down old, carefully curved ramp. Deserted granary, covered ramp running out over water, smell of sea.

Mudflats. Green path running down, wooden bridge over stream, birds singing. Old trucks at beginning of path. Junk and antiques everywhere. Wet branches, chlorophyll, bright green leaves and branches, red. All I do is think of you. If you came on to me this hard I'd run, but you promised not to or no you didn't. I agreed to your rules and you are not told mine so there you go and I'm gone too.

He's furry, covered with soft golden hair. The life of the open mind is never peaceful it seems. But it is passionate. It speaks about instincts, intuitions which transcend rationality.

Eros … guts … love's a deep word … easily muffed … and

muffed's a word to turn on too ... two ... me and you ... spectres over shoulder ... blend into a rider of proportions which can't be missed ... mist ... and a reality so hard it throws me into a further life where fire becomes a curious kind of delight full light ...

THE TRAIL THROUGH

The day mild, overcast, hung in its web of possibilities with a suspension of past, and all its ways open to the new. A childhood could vanish on such a day. Yet nothing might happen unless one was primed inside, waiting for such a lull wherein new understandings might break forth.

Hanna at sixteen, intensely aware of all she must be without knowing how to realize herself. Seeking social means to bolster her internal doubts. Throwing, outward and away, loves she should have kept for herself to fertilize her budding understandings.

Strength builds strength while in dissolution we will float away. Yet her whole inclination was to follow the crowd, if only she could find a way. Difficult this way was for first, the crowd must be found, then studied, then copied, and the life soon went out of living in all that invention and dissection.

Appearances were a primary problem. Hair once combed was fine combed fifty times, which she did and the strands became irritated, fell limp in exhaustion, covered themselves in protective grease. One look in the mirror would fulfill her need if only she could learn to stop at that, lose her greed, and pass on to the rest of her life in the same way.

This day dawned and hung, as Vancouver days will, between any particular kind of weather, full of life yet still. A perfect day to pass on beyond the details, the dead ends, establishing more fruitful routes for further practice.

A day demanding new action, when her hair combed out well on the first try and she was miles away from her prairie home on holiday. Far from home yet still tied, sitting on her grandparents' porch, dreaming of tales to tell her friends. And imagining her parents who, without knowing why, would suddenly realize that she had become an adult. Dressing with care, she discovered that new gait, that tilt and tension of body, belief in face which gives us grace.

Faced outward towards the world, she only knew of presenting newfound grace to adventures as books told of them, involving herself with new people, seeking success in an outside distant place. Later she would learn how to open to grace when it came and turn inward, cultivating it further within the world of herself.

Carrying herself carefully she kissed her grandmother goodbye and headed towards the whitened towers of the city. When she reached the city's centre she stepped off the downtown bus. She passed through the city crowds, smartly dressed rushing around the courthouse, in and out the huge Vancouver Hotel, their arrivals and departures glittering with speed and wealth in the pale day. She felt no separation from them of jealousy or doubt, the grace in her lent her their wealth as she passed on her way towards the art gallery where, she felt, she could see today what was beneath the surface there. Where the meaning lay, in the art, and in the people surrounding it.

Her trip became happy, the still haze could not cloud her delight. She smelled the green clippings of grass lawn freshly cut in front of the cathedral and felt the flitting leaves on the thin sidewalk trees. Birds sang to her in the heart of the city harmonizing with traffic in the wind which always whipped around this particular corner. Crossing the street she passed parking lots seeming to be great sculpture courts and vacant lots blooming with glorious, dogged weeds.

Entering the gallery the chill overawed her, the huge glass doors appeared to her as telescopes, anyone from anywhere on earth could watch her actions. Her happiness slipped. It ripped in two, one shred was doubtful and the other shred became unrecognizable, a mysterious watcher to whom the first, her doubtful self, must cater without knowing what would bring approval.

Then the paintings seized her attention pulling her up out of a rubble of confusion. The woman in her appeared, sensually responding to the deep, green sweeps of an Emily Carr canvas. She moved through the gallery of these forest paintings painted by a woman who had lived alone, giving herself up to the silent coast forest so she might, in its nature, find her own upon the canvas. The natural forces fed those in Hanna, who responded with all her growing awareness.

Trails led through the forest of these paintings, through wind-laden trees, deep shadows, tall cathedral clearings. Hanna felt the wild movement of the branches of an elemental orchestra and the drying power of the unique totems on a changing coastline. The possibilities of Hanna's life grew, rooted, deepened.

A man appeared standing at the doorway, she turned her gaze on him full of her newfound understandings. Able at last to meet a man as a man, to meet his eyes with her own as she stood there, a creature solidly part of this earth, where each action fulfills itself in the power of its own meanings.

The man wore a trench coat, smoked a cigarette, had peaked eyebrows and black hair, she noticed. He opened his mouth, started talking to her. "Would you tell me where the airlines bus depot is? She wants to go there," he said, indicating a young woman standing beside a suitcase near the huge glass doors.

"Oh I don't know," Hanna told him. Then he turned and asked the receptionist who showed him the bus depot through the doors directly across the street.

"He asked me! Why did he ask me?" Hanna wondered, intensely interested. She watched the man and woman leave, looked straight at him, returned his gaze when he looked back while holding the door open.

Where had she come from, this woman Hanna, who would meet an unknown man so boldly from across a room? She watched while he left. Then she turned and was carried into the paintings again.

She followed the trail of the forest, of the rooting of the trees, of the secret movements of the shadows around the room again, then crossed the hall and walked downstairs to the washrooms. The forest feeling carried over from the paintings and within the smells of green soap and disinfectant she could detect the earthly smells of cedar, excrement, and her own salty body. Avoiding the temptation to examine herself in the mirror too closely she washed her hands and, turning to leave, passed the far wall of the pale-yellow washroom. An etching of a Haida totem pole faced her. Detailed careful drafting, then the powerful features of a totemic man, meticulously reproduced, came to life. The original power of totem life sprang upright in the heavy rounded squat pole, a dark lucid phallus which carried her up the stairs to where the man, who had come in again, stood before a painting.

She just looked at him with nothing to say for she had never known life was like this. Lost in amazement and curiosity her doubts and question remained submerged. Her usual actions suited to her school friends or family could not find foothold. Her daydreams fell back restrained, to then later exult in the background: "A real adventure! A real romance!"

"I came back to see you," he said. "She's caught her bus now. Let's get some coffee." She followed him out the door. In his wrinkled trench coat and face he appeared to her a dramatic figure. She saw him as she saw Humphrey Bogart in the movies or Albert Camus in a publicity picture standing in a Paris doorway of chipped granite blocks and moss, collar open as was that of the man beside her, in the mild grey day.

Now he seemed shocked, "You're not just sixteen! You look older," he said. How the day, the grace, the Indigenous wood could change everything! Before all this, people had thought her less than her age.

There beside the strong paintings she could feel her own power coming from a common ground of feeling which could create a work of art or a glance. So she felt no fear in flirting, in her game, but delighted in its flow and in her first female adventure. Now the impetus from that first realization wound down and she must find fresh springs wherein to renew her faith in her womanly mission. Then she realized enough to be silent, with only a short question or two. Strange couple wooing each other only to satisfy curiosity.

"I'm a newspaper reporter," he told her. She seemed amazed at the thought. What did he do? "Well, interview all kinds of people. Exciting, yes, and a lot of work."

Their journey passed in fits and starts, a long way to the

department store restaurant. Each time that they slowed and panic appeared, she asked another question and became engrossed in his answer.

Sitting in the cafeteria overlooking the city he told her, "I really am a puppet master, I make puppets and perform with them. That way I'm entirely independent. I'll just work here on the newspaper until my funds become sufficient to finance my puppet theatre. Then I'll travel all over. Near at first, around the Northwest, then anywhere. The world will be open when I get going."

He seemed most pleased to tell her about his ambition. Their meeting had now reached its height, looking through the open grilled window beside their little table, the towers of the city appeared to her to wave like trees in the slight late-afternoon breeze.

Then his interest turned on her, pressed closer, she became nervous. More and more she felt a strangeness all around, here sitting with all these eating people whom she'd never know.

Sounds of traffic increased, rush-hour crowds building up added to her tensions. As evening came, the day grew more overcast and pressure of internal questions threw similar clouds over their encounter.

She felt a rising inside her, her hands slipped on her cup, something inside herself, or in the air all around them, moved them both, agitated that they leave, and so quickly they rose and only took the fire stairs down because he said, "That elevator must be the city's slowest!"

Pausing just before the ground floor he asked her why she had to leave so soon. She said, "I have to go, to go home to help Grandma with dinner," and rushed to board her bus. But she didn't really know why she had to go.

MAY 17

Married to no one and anyone. High priestess or courtesan, empress or whore. Hi to Jasmine, the mad cat who stalks around the garden. Poetry goes more slowly, may be written by fools, wholly ones we hope.

Would you please standardize your plot. I would if I could. If it were possible in 1970 to ignore that part of the rest of the world which comes knocking on your door. The Jehovah's Witnesses came yesterday.

I want empirical information about meditation. Other things too so long as the information relates. Relate; gets along well with relatives and other clannish individuals.

Yellow journalism all of it, we are scoundrels from the day we give up our masochistic bounds.

Adonis Adamus, animus, marriage to no one and anyone. Spread-eagled on gold velvet, on Librium, on the fine white line through black empty night. Though nothing is empty, of course. Gentle titter from the ladies' corner.

Sometimes all you hear is the man's story or the women's story. That doesn't make sense though. Glen says that there are mushrooms with four sexes.

Things slowing down. Just want to note that once you've met your true love you'll see him in many a face. And that this is being typed while sitting in a lotus position.

EARLY ONE MORNING

Christmas at the Stella Hotel. Run down, crummy, hideaway for gentle people crushed by the city machine, others twisted by drugs or alcohol, artists, non-alike except that they didn't "fit in." Stella Hotel and Boxcar Betty's annual Christmas dinner coming up.

Boxcar Betty was Hanna's friend. Not through any mutual concern, simply: There they were, two souls who recognized each other through the sea of blank faces and its undertow of despair.

Maybe Betty was sixty. She'd had one heart attack, her ankles kept swelling and she wouldn't slow down. She loved to tell of how once she was crowned Queen of the Vagrants. Several weeks before she had said to Hanna:

"Honey, why you hanging around here? If I had your looks, was twenty-one again, I'd go everywhere, my I'd do wild things! Why don't we go on the road together, ah I'd like to travel again."

Hanna didn't take it seriously, couldn't dream Betty's dreams, or even her own.

Skinny girl, beige hair short, capped to head, glasses, movements alternately graceful then awkward when tension chopped them off. Hanna couldn't go on the road, couldn't act anymore except huddle in her room all fall, sick. She'd desperately grabbed this time, thought she could use it, find herself, produce something she could believe in. Instead, questions, gloom piled up over her head until she couldn't make a movement in the world. Then slowly realized she must do something, take a step towards life, people, or she'd slip impossibly far away.

The Stella Hotel had no heat, except electric heaters. Your bill went up three dollars every week when you had one. Sometimes they'd all go on at once, blowing the fuses. Mrs. Wo the proprietress took this as an excuse to search each room for contraband appliances.

Hanna tried to concentrate, write in her cold room, but felt pursued by the icy wind whipping through bare, warehouse-lined sheets and down the light funnels of the hotel.

There was commotion downstairs, usually it was safer not to investigate but this time she could hear it was Betty. She got up, went out into the drafty hall. Betty was wandering around the lower corridor in curlers, slippers, muttering to herself, explaining her arrangements to whoever would listen.

"Honey, I've ordered a twenty-pound turkey from that cheap meat market on Market Street and I'm going down there now to pick it up."

"I'll go with you and help you carry it," Hanna said. Betty stopped in her doorway, amazed. "Oh you needn't do that, dearie."
"But I want to, Betty."

So they went. Day before Christmas, crowds were intense. Dark already at four o'clock. Somehow the bright lights made the grey buildings seem even bleaker. All the bars open, packed with hard-faced people, spilling out onto multicoloured streets. Tinsel illusion and city actuality at ragged right angles.

The bird was heavier than they'd expected. Twenty-four pounds of frozen turkey, block of ice in a double shopping bag.

"We'll take turns." Hanna didn't really see how Betty could have carried it alone. Her ankles swelling with each step, heels of her shoes worn down so outside of feet scuffed pavement, puffing, talking continuously. Hanna kept the turkey to herself.

"Carrying this bag keeps me warm."

Wind tore at them, street dirt blew up. Lights glittered through dust and chill, beautiful to see, Betty's chatter happy since someone might be listening, a mile maybe, each step closer to home.

Christmas afternoon, Betty must have worked all night to get the dinner ready. Everyone sitting down, packed into the grease-lined lower-floor kitchen. The room filled, once each year, with rich smells of good food. Even Mrs. Wo in attendance. Charlie with his careful concern helping Betty serve. Tattered Christmas wreaths above the table. Cynical giggles, sporadic attempts at gaiety, spirit finally coming through. Each shell of loneliness cracking slightly, then the cheer reeling off slightly into hysteria as the wine went down.

Sitting there Hanna could feel cramps creeping up on her, strange bands crisscrossing her belly. "Maybe too much food?" Stomachache grew until finally:

"Betty, excuse me, I've got to go."

And Betty, funny little curls askew, red cheek veins ready to burst, was drunk enough now that she didn't notice.

Upstairs, pains coming on. "If only the whole place hadn't been so dirty. The bathroom, oh God." She couldn't even go and sit there. Just crouch on her bed and wait. Maybe they'd go away.

Finally she admitted that all this was serious. "Why didn't you go to a doctor when you first missed your period? Why didn't you look after yourself? Even the most primitive can take care of their own bodies. Fool, fool, too late. Must do something. And here it wasn't so easy as at home. Money. Fifteen dollars a visit. But now imagine what the hospital will cost. You should have got a job. Paid for cleanliness, common sense. But I wanted time and did nothing. It's too late, must take care of it now, can't get rid of this pain myself."

"Davey said he'd drop by. When he comes I'll ask for a ride. I'll go to the country hospital. They'll take me and clear all of this up." But how long might it be before he came? Finally she phoned and left a message for him that she needed to see him, needed a ride.

Crouch, crouch and wait. "Why not go yourself, alone?" No nerve left, only these convulsions, a trip to the filthy toilet.

That night, late, Charlie at the door. Funny Charlie, or maybe not so funny.

"Just wanted to know if you'd like a cup of coffee." Pause. "Are you all right?"

She could hardly talk to him. "Musn't show there's anything wrong."

Charlie with his huge glasses and perpetual look of concern.

Crouch and rock all that night, the next day passed in a faster blur. Five that evening and she realized, "Davey won't come. He hasn't got the message. He doesn't understand, he's in trouble himself. He cares, but not enough. He's not going to come."

Downstairs she could hear activity beginning in the kitchen. "Charlie's just getting home from work."

She met him on the stairs, asked for a ride. Said she wasn't feeling well.

"But have your supper first, it's no emergency."

She could just barely look at his face, his glasses shining therein. Twenty-watt light bulb, dark red and dirt-carpeted hall.

Charlie, someone acting at last. A ride through dark, wet streets. No small talk, what could they say? She drifted away. Parking. A huge grey building, prison fence, three blocks of institution.

Inside, bedlam. Not even a hospital. Drunk folks reeling, children screaming, blood flowing, activity flooding through the bright emergency waiting room. Stretchers rushed back and forth while the lineups didn't move at all.

"Charlie, thank you, maybe you'd better go."

"I'll wait for just a while."

He wouldn't leave, waited through that long hour or more. At last an intern with his sheaf of papers. Charlie, seeing someone taking her, could go. She felt very alone as she watched the huge doors swing shut behind him.

"And I didn't realize he was a friend until I had to ask for help."

The intern, clean-shaven, blond, serious, speared her with questions.

"Name, occupation?" Not bad. Then.

"The father?"

She didn't want to tell.

"He's not coming," she said.

Finally the intern wrote: "Unknown."

"Where did you have the abortion?"

"It's not an abortion."

He didn't believe her. She thought she'd scream. Rationally it didn't matter, but his assumption horrified her because it wasn't true. They thought she was lying.

He wrote a few more words down and left. An hour passed. Two white coats came with a stretcher, took her into one of the curtained rooms. Poked and prodded and twisted her on her pain.

"It looks like four months."

Someone gave her a pill, left.

A blur, movement, voices, cold hallways passing by, icy smell of ether, crisp sheets. Another pill.

Back bent and turning, something inside which had to come out and hung on and on.

Her body wouldn't move.

Her mind shrieked.

She pushed, willed weight, groaned out loud. Nurse came and spoke to her.

"Now stop it, you're distracting the other women."

Retching helped also, shook her stomach. A nurse came again.

"You'll throw up that pill and it's to cause contractions. The uterus is infected and the walls won't move as they should."

Alone. Silence. Pressure, ache, something inside, a dead weight that must come out. She could feel it had to be removed but didn't know how to make it go.

Waves of cramps and that lump through it all.

Breathing with the pain helped. Deep, deep breath into the lump.

Through the blur a pattern began to develop. Her body started moving, her breath with it. Careful, don't interfere. The distress and pressure mounted, became a single perception. Effort, concentration, sucked her in until she became the rhythm. Huge waves.

Suddenly she was gone, a consciousness emerged beyond it all, just enough to say: "Careful, don't move."

Her body, waves of movement continued, finally organically meshed and that spot of clarity where her memory remained watched in awe.

Her body, moved on the pulses, mounted the building pressure. Finally something moved inside.

A soft flow into the bedpan.

The pressure was gone.

She lay there a long time, then she looked. Floating in its sea of blood and clear amniotic fluid, a soft dark body, rocking gently as if on edge of lapping waves, a tiny sea creature, hands and feet perfectly formed. "Beautiful creature, not dead or alive but existing in some prehistoric state, before we were separate from the sea and love."

A nurse bustled by, checking. Looked in at Hanna and realized what had happened. Quickly grabbed the bedpan and its precious contents. A few seconds later Hanna could hear the pan dumped in the sterilizer. Clatter, flush. Gone. A great emptiness everywhere, then sleep.

Next morning, a flow in her waking, sun colours in eyes before they open. Voices muttering gently, clean smells, antiseptic hospital. Yellow curtains on the windows, changing grey light to sun colours, gold reflections off the white beds. "Open my eyes to the morning and I'm happy, I don't know why, to be alive." Recollecting the baby, ache in marrow of bones, crying and then remembering how it carried love. "All that can happen despite my confusion, doubt. Now I know life's real: Those powers inside moved me when my mind had given up. Now this in me will grow while I'm alive. Wake up, wake up, the day seizes me, much to do, make sure now, the next baby, if I'm given one, has a chance to grow."

JUNE 3 (NEW MOON)

[...] Sitting here with the radio on and the news brings the world on. Our premier who rules this province as a heavy dictator talking about the nations of the Pacific Rim and the Prime Minister says he will put forward a bill which could remove the illegality of abortion in one day. Women's Liberation stand on street corners asking for this every weekend. Political organizations bore and stifle me yet sometimes they fit the moment, lift the gnawing of deadly realities into significant movement.

Some days are like that too, everything comes together at once and all you worked for so doggedly and blindly sometimes comes true.

JUNE 19 (FULL MOON)

Writing is maybe something we do to preserve sanity, to finally make the story real in a bigger sense than it was to start with. That can be taken as a pragmatic statement and a metaphysical one [...]

Watching the sunset this evening, waves rocking up at my folded legs, the light over the ocean seemed to surround me. There is a particular luminous quality about the sunsets on this coast. The sky cleared today, and it was the first visible sunset for a week. The Italian fishermen were out in hip waders inspecting their smelt nets. I looked around at the beautiful young men walking down the beach, my eyes going out to them discovering the almost perfect natural urges present. I looked for you but you weren't there.

[...] I've been sitting here feeling some kind of life well up in me. Greg would say, "You're just horny." As I write this, a cat howls a mating yodel just outside the window, and I remember it is a full moon tonight. Or is it? Not quite reached its ultimate yet, the solstice will be upon us within a week. And then there is that particularly high summer tide.

Myths have always come to me. Usually when I am very alone, when any inner remembrances start coming to me. And now there is a man around who comes to me sometimes but still leaves me free. And what but that doesn't really drive a woman mad or leave the way open for her to discover her obsession, her insanity?

Or maybe this story stretched back to Egypt when it was Alexandria, Gnostic centre. There was a woman of impeccable style who wrote about a palimpsest of lives and loves, stretching over twenty-two centuries. So I am giving you people who live both in life and in dream. I will give them to you as I can as they have come to, and left me, flowing or broken, in and out of my vision. Some always on the periphery, some bursting in at the centre and then leaving as they came and some just barely always there, but existing in their continuity.

And then there is Greg who ties together myth and reality. Maybe that's all we ever want: some bridge between dream and reality.

[...] I had a long series of dreams before I met Bartolome. The thought frightens me when I think about it. My hand falters on the keys for the whole thing is beginning to become clear.

The series of dreams first taught me to swim and then how to fly. It's funny, when you are in the middle of these things you usually don't notice what is happening, but submerged in the events continue on as if blind or as a skin diver in deep water, moving very slowly through a thick gorgeous element, but one that is not quite your own.

In these dreams, which continued throughout several weeks, building up a bit more each night, I was, at first, floating on the surface of a vast muddy river. Then I had fallen into this river from a bridge that jutted straight out from a huge city, hung with freeways, into a narrows.

Then I was no longer floating on the river but fighting for my life, keeping myself from submerging. For nights my struggles with the river went on until I managed to catch hold of floating debris. Finally I learned to navigate on a body-sized raft. After that, the raft disappeared, and I was navigating unconscious of support on the raging river.

Some short time later I was running in a huge fallow field

outside a flat Saskatchewan town. There were gliders in the sky above me. Sometimes the sky was that wide-open bright-blue prairie sky, sometimes clouds would cover the sun utterly and the weather would become dark, ominous and overcast. The gliders were at first always in sight and I was running with the wind in my ears to try to catch them. Once or twice as I stretched myself out towards them my hand would almost touch one. Then I began to concentrate on my form in running, gather my intention, my belly, my guts and cunt. The lower part of my body became attuned to my desire. At last I found that if that part of me was synchronized with my will as I ran, I rose up off the earth and almost became one of the gliders. I remember now that at one point I was even diving and swooping through telephone and powerlines and looking into the eyes of some strange soft hawk. But if my intention faltered at all, if my attention strayed, I would be again left alone in my doubts and would fall terribly back to ground. Sometimes I would start gradually to fall and would fight to find the vital clue within myself, the power to keep me off the ground. The sensation was delightful, and slowly I learned to isolate it and even use it in my outward life. But like most of us I was only too ready to use it instead of work with it and gradually I forgot what I learned.

One night as a young girl she went to sleep. As she lay sleeping she dreamed of a deep valley and satyrs played in it. She watched them from afar and finally ran to join them. As she came closer she lost sight of them, for the lift of a hill in front of her obscured her vision. She then had to continue through the underbrush for a long way before she met any sign of them. The first indication that she had that they were still around was the rhythm of their hoofbeats through the ground. She could leave now she realized for the hoofbeats sounded loud and strong and made her heart pound, but she also knew that once you leave a dream you can't come back. Unless of course it's next time around. So she stayed. Wandered down into the green valley, passed the aspens and poplars until she reached the grassy meadowlands where a small stream tinkled through. Somewhere off in the shadows there was the smoke of tobacco burning. Suddenly out of the poplars at the head of the small grove, they came. She stood frozen. All held back but one which advanced towards her. She swayed, held by ecstasy and fear. Again she remembered this was a dream and that if she wished she could leave. But instead she let him come near. A dream will flee as quickly as a deer. Soon he was so close she could see herself in his eyes. As they met she thought, since he can come into me this way he can come back into the real world through my eyes.

Her bedroom was dark and built of long-stained shiplap. An attic room. Ceiling hipped to fit the roof.

BARTOLOME

She met him in Seattle, fifteen years after that dream. On a bus in the loading zone of the Seattle bus station, where it was reloading for San Francisco. She was on her way there after months of waiting and filling in of endless visa forms. She was full of a marvellous sense of freedom at this point, that feeling that with some effort she could go anywhere, do anything she wanted to do.

Then he got on the bus and his eyes looking at hers were the eyes from the dream. He was that man, creature, only he had on quite ordinary clothes and instead of hooves he limped a little. Most people would only notice that he was darker than many of the passengers, wore a woolly Afghan hat, and was carrying a huge, glossy book of the prints of Hieronymus Bosch.

So there was the glance as he came on the bus and then as he sat down beside her, a rhythm sprang up between them. The tone and rise and fall of his voice reached through her ears to her guts and she became aware of the sensation of his flesh almost touching hers. Their breath synchronized spontaneously.

He sat beside her, sealing off the rest of the bus, off the world from their charmed circle. A current passed between them. The ease of his company was astonishing, in fact all the time behind their encounter there was the air of a magical event, which delighted her but also surrounded the edges of her mind with a constant air of disbelief.

Sitting together on the bus. Sometimes she would get breathless and then she would have to draw back and stop forcing the companionship. Yet quickly after she withdrew she felt her attention pulled towards him, their attention pulled together, magically.

They looked through his book for a long time, fell under the spell, and when they got to Portland they got off the bus together.

As soon as she got off the bus and agreed to leave the depot, go with him, spend some time, maybe the night, she became very nervous, and somewhat unaware too, for her ticket was straight through to San Francisco so she lost twenty dollars of it right there. Maybe she was possessed, any explanation will do.

So they went and had a drink which calmed her down a bit and then headed towards a hotel.

He was dark and to her eyes very gorgeous. Who knows what other people see? He said he was part Irish and part Puerto Rican and the rest, Black maybe. What a woman sees in a man and what men see, too, is that energy. A way of moving. Where the blood comes up to the surface of the skin. Smells almost indecipherable, undetected by the mind, pull us. His eyes were there and later she remembered the way he kept looking at her.

So crawl into another's arms, turn in bed in love feel another body. A long time sleeping alone. Soft movement of flesh on flesh. To share this close, bodies speaking their own language. Flow of movement, then the pressure of flesh in the stillness creating another movement, and that returned. Touch moving touch, mind suffused with sensation. Until movement's then an entity, carrying two together into hidden paths where pleasure's energy grows.

Dreaming true. Living where there is no more questioning.

"You're like a snake when you curl around." She was freer than she had ever been, moving on a current of sense. He watched her, could hold himself back until he found where they next should go. Given herself, given both, and more depth than she had ever known.

Following curves of sensation, delicate shivers, widening out. Waiting. Still. Now another unfolding of muscles, sinew, and flesh. Lyric, song, music, dance of Gods, colours glow.

Eyes open, and his eyes open first, watching, fathomless, an enigma, yet body as close as my own.

At one time during the long evening she woke up to the visible reality and his eyes were looking straight into hers, as if he could see everything about her.

They became two bases of energy. The rhythms, more intense. Concentration. Moving together as one organism, stretched between the two ends of the universe. Flying on the impulse of double spirals of delight. And suddenly emerging out of sensation into emptiness. Boundaries gone. Space. Gone, gone, gone beyond, gone altogether beyond.

So this was it, given and even now fading, something was drawing her back and she wanted to stay, to hold on to nothing. Light and dark began to separate out, differentiate. Light spots, like dust motes in empty black, stars in the universe, she named them. Energy of separated objects maybe, or the character of her eye. A voice was pulling her back now. He was saying something. If she opened her eyes, the last remnants would go away.

Move, that's what he wants. OK. Shocked to find that that space had been something else for him. Flipping from open to closed like a sea anemone in several seconds, heavy armour clicking into place around her as she moved off him.

The next day she woke up and looked at him. Then looked around the room, a terrific nervous tension grasped her guts. She had no idea who he was or where they were. For a second she thought she'd drown in the strangeness of it all.

Woke up in the morning totally new. "No no no no no no no no no no no."

"Give me a story, please."

Dreams, colours fading, turning, warm next. Smells of sex, soft cushion, a body next to her. "Don't examine it all too closely. Don't lose the dream." Questions flooding in. An edge of terror, prickling under the armpits. "Back, back into the dream." Colours again. "I remember, out in space, blackness all around, and spots of light, stars."

"Hey, you're awake."

"Ignore that voice, feel flesh ignore consciousness. Striving for orientation first. Find a strong warm base."

The sunlight coming in. Drifting off into another dream, half remembered. She hung on to sleep. Then as a trick of her mind, awake. Eyes open looking around. Close them again and drift off but it was useless. Awake.

"What am I doing here?" Strange plush hotel room. Flick of nerves. Terrible tension. Sounds of vacuum in the hall, traffic noises from street below. Stomach contracting. He got up. Transitions are so hard to face. Quick get your clothes on. Make the bed. Do all those normal things.

Sitting on the bed ready to go when he came back in. From stranger into closest intimate and back to now a stranger, an unknown face. What to do? Should they just get up and leave. He was a lot easier, maybe he did this every day. He was glowing. A beautiful man. But her only knowledge of him was sensual and that of a dream. Their lives so separate that there seemed no way to relate except by what the body knows. There was no more reason to be in this place. Maybe we should eat. The disorientation was complete. Some knowledge of acting would have helped or a recourse to the spirit if only she had known. But all there was was a leap that had been taken. A black void floating behind, some strange memories. When she pushed her mind back to it there was a rush of joy and the curious space. The sheet was torn. You did that with your leg he said. She looked at it in amazement – she didn't even remember. She could hardly remember anything.

They sat together. Slow conversation. He told her a bit of his life but she couldn't concentrate. She had pretended to know what was going on and now she'd found herself out.

"You're beautiful you know," he said. "I've never met anyone like you." Maybe he meant it. He seemed really excited. "I've some money that was left me by my grandmother in New York. I don't have to work even. I'll wire the bank and get some more. Let's just take off together." She looked at him. She couldn't believe the stories of money. A part of her disapproved. She didn't want any plans. They all seemed peripheral. She couldn't give the magic free flow, could hardly take in what he was saying. Didn't believe him. He was a phantom who had come up into her life, how could she make plans when she hardly knew his name. Her mind flew round and round. He stopped, puzzled. "What's wrong?" he asked. "Don't you want to come with me? You're free, aren't you?" And now she knew she wasn't, not really, because she couldn't let herself go anymore. All she could feel were desperate movements of withdrawal. Now he was getting hurt. "There are greener pastures somewhere else, is that it?" he asked.

"Oh no." She wanted to cry. "I just wish I was at home." But now she didn't even know where her home was. Somehow she couldn't go back into the dream nor could she go forward into what seemed to be reality.

"Look I've never met anyone like you before. I want to get to know you. Come with me."

She went out to get some food and pick up some things from her bags at the bus depot. The city was steaming hot and frightening in its metallic sheen. Gaudier and brighter than her home. All her nerves were unfolded, open, and too easily absorbed the harsh, glittering space.

He had some business to do, he said, but he wouldn't tell her what it was, went out to meet someone she didn't get to see. He was strangely secretive. They spent a nervous day. Finally she said she was leaving. He didn't fight her on it any longer, but accompanied her to the bus depot silently. They had some time to put in before the bus was to come and after sitting again in silence he said he had a phone call to make. He was gone a long time. The bus loaded and still she waited. Finally it was to pull out, she paid for her ticket a second time and gave it to the driver. She had a sudden suspicion that he had deliberately gone away. Should she wait? So she got on the bus, all the time imagining him appearing as the bus left, nerves driving her at a terrific pace. The bus pulled out, as it rounded the corner in the crowd at the edge of the pavement she fancied for a moment that she saw his face.

JULY 10

The days now pass like lightning, like wildfire, and return me to a place I've never been. So we slowly creep on our way to no place in particular, tracing the lineaments of our dream. "Where are you going, child?" "I don't know, Mother, could you show me where to go?" "Sorry little one, but where you are going no one ever knows. And they, even less than you, know where you have been. You have been wandering in that dark wood for a long while, why don't you give up the fight? Why not come out into the light? Greet the day of new life. Constantly awake and reawake in my arms. Ignore the world of men and their rationality. What they do not know is that the sun is alive and it feeds you and me. You have chosen a hard road. To make the despair and the joy conscious. Tell tales not yet told and when you tell them they won't be believed.

New language is necessary, but not recognized. Few hear what they are told constantly. Few dare go where they are led by their nose but wait instead in a steady mire of disbelief. But ignore them, you have listened too long. Why not strike out for yourself. Now I know you think this madness, I know you don't know where to go, or how to grow and believe the gestalt."

JULY 12

All that interests me is the revelationary aspect of a work. There is disalignment. Revelation may be essentially quiet and not in the least dramatic, especially to one brought up in our insidiously tense and violent culture.

Here I am balanced between despair and delight. The delightful world outside my window and the one inside my own body, almost as if a state of ecstasy were inherent in my body but I seldom noticed it. Or maybe passing waves of its presence. Why does one worship pleasure so? Is there really such a thing as abstract meaning? Ultimately, introspection is for pragmatists too. And no one wants to believe in God unless they feel that presence. God's a dangerous word to use, I realize [...]

So midsummer has come and gone, we are on the downward

side of the cycle. The I Ching says, "In the fifth month the element begins its ascent again and the creative is on the wane."

The air is sultry, the sun is hot but the day is overcast. The city is bound by strikes. Harbour full of huge ships waiting for cargo which has not come. Mail is not coming through. I went to the post office this morning and she sold me stamps and then said, "They tell us to warn you not to put your mail in the box for no one is responsible for it right now."

Even the prices of meat might fall, the sales are beginning and people are trying to dig in. We all need cheaper places to live and they are not available. Art is a supreme luxury perhaps but may be a recourse to meaning throughout it all.

When we first made love this spring it seemed the whole world was alive. Greg, who insists on being first an animal, called it a seasonal thing which I could not see in my romantic dream, yet when we made love last, just after midsummer, on the first day of the fall, the energy had changed. We are aged in it already. Do we have a grace which moves us outside of this? That seemed apparent too and is the only reason I can write this at all.

AUGUST 19

So at last I get to the place where I am just going to have to accept all the conditions of my existence. Clumsy, messy though they may be. Here I am at Storm Bay sitting in front of Matty's cabin. Brown rice cooking on the Coleman stove, stinking the air, and it doesn't matter. I am rapidly becoming a slob and don't care. Sitting typing on Maxine's Hermes typewriter, a beautiful machine although I am hindered by the tab setting. This world of machines often stymies me. I guess we learn eventually to face the things which we have up until then been avoiding. Like this life of mine. Pay attention to the simple things and friends and family.

Words words, a petty imitation of the real.

Four days after the high moon the tide seems to change. So I have managed to get out of town, and really away from him again and I won't even admit to myself what all of this feels like, for I have a long way to go before it runs out.

So we start from the same, proceed till we are cleared. No one is guilty, we all do what we can, everyone is helpful as they can be, everyone gave something to me. It seems this is just the way it had to be. So long as I am working it is OK. Now I hear the boat coming back in. The changes are difficult to comprehend. The mosquitos get bad as soon as I stop work. What has been happening is the last leap in a long trend. We give credit to our friends.

I didn't think I would be writing like this when I got out here, I thought I would learn something new, instead I just think about you. Apollo. Dionysus, that in us which is of God is in everyone. My Quaker aunt was here last week from Philadelphia. When the gossip was exhausted she said just a little about her faith. When I asked her if God could be interpreted in Spirit she said, "Quite."

Left my work early and came up here to learn how to use a canoe. It seems that up here you can do just about anything you want. Concentrate equally on all things and you will be free. Attention and attitude. This keeps singing me to sleep in the little voices of the wood. Don't say anything phony. Who can speak with authority. From the belly please. So much to learn. Doing what comes naturally. When the sun goes down we will all have a feast and be easy. Meanwhile, the mosquitos bite and someone is out there swimming, the sounds pull me.

AUGUST 20 MAYBE … I DON'T KNOW.

The time changes in this place … Things move in similar ways to the city but I am left behind somehow. I hope this isn't my paranoia day today for I have work to do.

Got to go chop some wood, the feast was incredible by the way. But now this morning I am cold.

In balancing is where the trick seems to be. Came up here easily, must help them remember neither to hang on nor throw away. Sitting not too far from the present moment. Hanging on to nowhere to go. Sighing like the wind in the trees.

The Continuous Present

1997

Three authors who used the continuous present: Gertrude Stein, Mickey Spillane, James Joyce; more recently it has been used by bill bissett and other friends of mine.

Visceralisations   a lot of the time *blewointment* was inclusive, not reductive; intelligent, not pedantic. Not much proofreading, spontaneous was the way. Pretty classy, phonetic spelling, line drawings, energy spilling off the pages.

Dance / a community rag   against the possibility of losing your voice. Hannah Wilkie said, "When people get so annoyed with the content that they refuse to look at things formally then it is necessary to continue."

At twenty we danced into the spider's web. Sunshine like today when bill gave me the first *blewointment*. I think it was during the '63 poetry conference at UBC.

Marge Piercy argues that poetry is deliberately censored in North America by means of ridicule and discreditation.

"The revolt of the 'haves'. In the recession of the '90s there has been virtually no drop in profits."

Involuntary poverty / against poverty of the mind   beyond the life force / rifting on the river / revisiting our vicissitudes.

blew ointment / blue sky / blue as coloured photocopy ink.

Oh Martina Clinton's poetry in issue #4!

> "... gosh they're really like
> Respighi those birds the orchestration
> they've got going – that huge yellow globe

> on top

of that tree
..."

I love rereading this poem!
It's a hard act to follow   poetry as primacy
blood sugar / ligature / survival
below – in a kind of touch of garlands never
extreme lace   extemporaneity panosomatic

In Defense of Maxine Gadd

2008

The reviewing of poetry books is a difficult job and your reviewer, Lyle Neff, appears to be serious about his work. Nevertheless, I must point out that his June 14 review of *Subway Under Byzantium*, by Maxine Gadd, misunderstood and underestimated Gadd's work.

He misunderstood three aspects: its humour, its "darkness," and its complexity. *Subway Under Byzantium* is a dense work that can be enjoyed on first reading but also repays several careful rereadings.

Gadd's humour is often satiric, witty, and underplayed. Her so-called dark visions are no more distressing than the world we live in and serve to illuminate and elucidate the political, social, and psychological complications facing us.

For the last century or so, literature has been involved with opening our narrative constraints, and Gadd doesn't ignore this. I urge each of you to discover her book's virtues for yourself.

Judith Copithorne
Vancouver

from

A Personal and Informal Introduction and Checklist Regarding Some Larger Poetry Enterprises in Vancouver Primarily in the Earlier Part of the 1960s

2010

Some time ago I began making a list of poetry events that took place in Vancouver in the decade of the 1960s. The list does not purport to be complete; I woke up one morning and wrote some of it as it came to my mind. As an introduction to the chronological list[1] and to try to make my intentions clear, I have included parts of these paragraphs that are entirely personal. They introduce my own emotional substance and explain why I wanted to make the list. The first part of the introduction partially describes some things that happened to me in the years from 1959 to 1963, when I had first come back to Vancouver. The second introductory part, which attempts to be fairly objective, comments on what I am trying to do with the list, and also upon a couple of larger poetry events in which I participated a little later in the sixties. Hopefully, there will soon be a more extensive and comprehensive study done of what I have begun to present here.

In writing this, my main wish is to indicate the breadth and variety of literary life in Vancouver proper in the 1960s, and I would like to thank all the many people who helped me gather information and edit this work. *Ocean/Paper/Stone*, a catalogue of some Vancouver literary publications written by Robert Bringhurst and published by the inimitable Bill Hoffer, was a useful resource.[2] The Vancouver Public Library was very helpful, as was the *BC Bookworld* author bank website.[3] I have used the Internet and have sometimes chosen one of several alternate dates that came from several different sources.

Looking back on that decade, I realize how exciting Vancouver seemed to me. The literary atmosphere was definitely lively.

---

1   Omitted here due to page constraints.

2   Robert Bringhurst, *Ocean/Paper/Stone* (Vancouver: William Hoffer, 1984).

3   www.abcbookworld.com/.

Many things seemed possible. I had come from Regina, Saskatchewan, and the size of the city of Vancouver was overwhelming to me, even though Vancouver was much smaller than it is now. Perhaps there is an optimum size for a city for certain sorts of interactions to occur. In those days, Vancouver was big enough to have a lively artistic scene, yet small enough for there to still be communication throughout many parts of it. There was a variety of bookstores and art galleries; there were art openings and poetry readings, which I had not experienced in Regina, where I had lived until 1958 when I made the move to Vancouver with my family.

One thing that tied my experiences together was the political aspect of my life. I had very little time or energy, but I did manage to go to a variety of political events and marches. When I did, I would also meet my literary friends there, which added another level to our experiences together. There were several intertwined aspects to the political activities that I found myself involved in. Without ranking them, these included the antiwar and peace movements, socialist activities, and feminism, which added a particular aspect to our activities.

Around 1961, I dropped out of university and worked at a number of jobs. A bit earlier than that, thanks to bill bissett's suggestion, I got to hear the unforgettable Kenneth Patchen accompanied by an awe-inspiring Al Neil. Then I got to meet Fred and Eve Douglas and Curt Lang, who would soon start the Radiant Bookstore which would later become MacLeod's Books. A bit before that, I was able to visit the beautiful Kaye's Books on Robson Street; I went several times with bill bissett, who was good friends with the Kayes. There was also the People's Co-op Bookstore, which had moved to Pender Street and was run in those days by Binky Marks.

Roy Kiyooka and his family were from Regina; I had met John Newlove in Weyburn, Saskatchewan, where I had worked as a nurse's aid in the mental hospital. So although I was new to Vancouver, I did already know people here in the arts and literary community. Both Roy and John had moved here not long after

I arrived with my family. Artists Brian Fisher (with whom I had gone through high school) and Claude Breeze (whom I had also known in Regina) had moved here not long after Roy did; he had been their professor at the Regina College Art School. I would meet all of them, mostly on Robson Street, at the library or (more often) at the Little Heidelberg Coffee House. I mention these people because their ideas, their friendliness, their quirks, and their activities inspired me.

During that time, I also got to visit San Francisco and spend time in City Lights Bookstore, which, it seems, many of the people mentioned here had also done. City Lights was one of the most exciting places I had visited at that point in my life.

The magazine *TISH* produced its first issue in 1961 and bill bissett produced the first issue of *blewointment press* in 1963. These two magazines, each in their own way, had a serious impact on the future of Canadian writing. The ideas espoused and the people they published are still active in Canadian writing today.

Then the 1963 Poetry Conference was held at UBC, and many famous poets spoke and read there. Sometimes referred to as the '63 Vancouver Poetry Conference, it attracted many people from Vancouver and elsewhere, including Charles Olson, Allen Ginsberg, Robert Creeley, Robert Duncan, Denise Levertov, Margaret Avison, and Philip Whalen. Many other people from Canada and the US were there as part-time speakers and full-time participants. The principal organizer was Warren Tallman. Tapes of this, made by Fred Wah, are available online at the Slought Foundation.[4] More information on this can be found in *Writing in our Time* by Pauline Butling and Susan Rudy.[5]

By this time, I had moved to North Vancouver which had a very poor bus service, especially at night. I seldom went out to late events in the city, but luckily I had a chance to go to the amazing Sound Gallery, created by Gregg Simpson, Al Neil, Sam Perry,

---

4   slought.org/resources/vancouver_1963.

5   Pauline Butling and Susan Rudy, *Writing in Our Time: Canada's Radical Poetries in English (1957–2003)* (Waterloo, ON: Wilfrid Laurier University Press, 2005).

and others. I performed there one night; soon, more and more people performed there. Helen Goodwin, who had been a mentor to many young women through her dance classes and workshops at UBC, soon joined in the activities. She then went to New York on sabbatical and when she got back, she set up Motion Studio on Seymour Street. Information about these activities can be found through Gregg Simpson's website.[6] Helen was the guardian angel of interdisciplinary art in Vancouver; she made a huge personal commitment in time, effort, money, and love to Motion Studio, as did the late Sam Perry.

Motion Studio lasted for less than a year, but a huge number of innovative activities took place there. Helen Goodwin had always been interested in an expanded view of the arts and included poetry in her dances. She let poetry lead off into a variety of activities, with help from Perry, Simpson, Neil and other remarkable artists, composers, electronics experts, and amazing innovators. At that time in the art world, the influence of pop art and conceptual art foregrounded the interactions of art and literature, while concrete and sound poetry were becoming better known in the literary world.

The year 1966 was, without doubt, the best and the worst of times. The war in Vietnam permeated everyone's minds; it broke through the usual barriers and filled the space around us with flames. Draft resisters arrived every day from the US. Meanwhile, there were activities and demonstrations, as well as the "be-in" organized by Jamie Reid that also included poetry. After that, the life of poetry in the city appeared to move in several different directions at once. I cannot report on them all, but I have tried to list the best known of the larger events.

One area that I am not able to report on fully enough is equivalent non-English speaking or non-European derived poetry events that might have taken place, or events that mainly involved poets whose primary heritage and interest were not Western European.

---

6   www.greggsimpson.com/.

Hopefully that lack will be better addressed in the next approach to this material. I have listed the Steveston Haiku Society, which lasted an amazing fifty years considering the small size of the community. When Japanese Canadians were sent to internment camps during WW II. This is the only group I have listed that did not primarily use the English language in their meetings, so far as I know. The Asian Canadian Writers' Workshop was formed sometime in the 1960s by the brilliant writer and powerful organizer Jim Wong-Chu and others.

II.

It might be seen as ironic that in regard to such a subjective discipline as poetry, I have used objective criteria for choosing the events I have listed. For more than one hundred years, it has been clear that the traditional forms of literary philosophy did not have a wide enough framework, field of possibility, or ideology to support much of what was being attended to in poetry. With this understood, there was then an open field or sphere of possibility available. Some people have chosen to be a part of one school, philosophy, or style, only to remain but part of it. For this list, I have chosen to make note of all speech or writing that called itself (or was called) "poetry," that had a larger, thoughtful audience within the parameters of Vancouver proper in the 1960s. By larger, I mean there was a sufficient number of people interested in it to ensure that the books or magazines publishing it were in demand and that the reading series or shows that featured it were consistently attended.

As for the question of Vancouver as the locale, this determination was as sufficient as any other geographical location and was not chosen in order to naively mythologize the locale for nostalgic or privileging reasons. I contend that if we are willing to look, we will see that "local" and "international" are intrinsically interrelated, with cycling energy and structural activities continuing much the way they do in the human body.

At the local level, the actions of people when aligned can be very productive. There was much of worth coming from the city. Poets, after all, are readers, carriers, and forwarders of intellectual, physical, and emotional information. The people in the city generated much inspiration, so that the poets of the city helped to produce the gestalt that made Vancouver so interesting.

There were a number of poetry readings by exceptional and prominent poets each year at UBC, and many exciting poets visited UBC in the 1960s. In the last years of the 1950s and the first few years of the following decade, there were readings by Langston Hughes, Marianne Moore, and Kenneth Patchen, as well as others. Leonard Cohen read at UBC at least twice during the 1960s, while M.C. Richards, Eli Mandel, and Margaret Avison read there at least once; Margaret Atwood taught there for a year. Earle Birney taught at UBC from 1946 to 1965, and it was primarily through his efforts that the Creative Writing Department at UBC was created. His powerful, innovative, and creative poetry and classes and his support and kindness inspired many younger poets and others.

Also, through the efforts and kindnesses of Warren and Ellen Tallman, a number of outstanding and boundary-breaking poets visited and read at UBC or sometimes in the city proper. Poets Allen Ginsberg, Robert Duncan, Michael McClure, Lew Welch, Basil Bunting, and Joanne Kyger visited several times in that decade. Robert Creeley taught at UBC for a year in 1962–1963; Robin Blaser moved and took up residence in Vancouver in 1966 and started teaching at SFU. His charisma, erudition, unsurpassed poetry books, classes, and readings inspired and nourished many people in Vancouver and elsewhere. The decade was an exciting time at the universities; I hope that someone will soon be able to make a more comprehensive study of this. I only studied at UBC for two years at the beginning of the sixties, so my personal information of what happened after that is limited. There are others who can do a good job of writing about activities at the universities. Much information about events at the universities is already archived, while events in the city proper do not have that amount of documentation, so this list serves this very particular purpose.

There have also been many important and communicative people, poets, teachers, and others in the city who have helped increase the level of our understanding, not all of whom I am able to mention due to constraints of time and space. As I have said, the emphasis here is entirely on city-level events. This may seem contradictory, but to my mind, it deals with a level of the poetry community that helped poets interact and grow. Regretfully, there is much I had to leave out, but I feel that the most important thing at this point for me is to give a small picture of one part of the life of poetry in this city at a particular point in time when it felt to me to be inspired as a whole.

It was not easy for women poets in early 1960s Vancouver. Maxine Gadd has always been one of the very best poets around. Her work, her performances, her feminism, and her imagination continue to fascinate me. Pat Lowther was another great and politically dedicated writer who was supportive of women; Beth Jankola and Anne McKay were each superb poets who offered me inspiration and friendship. There were other exceptional women, some of whom were writers and artists, and some who had quite different interests. I met and became familiar with the varied and brilliant work of Phyllis Webb, Dorothy Livesay, Myra Macfarlane, Marya Fiamengo, Gwen Hauser, Daphne Marlatt, Nellie McClung, and Skyros Bruce/Mahara Allbrett. During this time, women also came from outside the city: the inimitable Margaret Atwood and Diane di Prima, who read with her company of performers, the Floating Bear; both gave exceptional readings here.

Each of these women's writing had quite different qualities. The work of some has been, for excellent reasons, well remembered; that of others has been undeservedly almost forgotten, but their struggles with the complexities of society formed an important support web in those days – for many people, including me. Each of the women mentioned were strong and talented; they commented on and explored the travails of women in our society, and were usually serious supporters of feminist ideas. As such, they were also involved in the battles being fought to forward the social and economic equality and physical and intellectual freedom of everyone. Feminism has always been an important facet of this movement and is almost inextricably intertwined with it.

There are many types of accuracy. I hope this loose compilation will jog some memories and produce further aesthetic and emotional recollections and reconstructions by others. The light in the city on a good day was phenomenal, doubtless due to the presence of water on three sides, the presence of many vacant lots full of undergrowth, and the mountains along the north. The illuminating photographs of Fred Herzog and Fred Douglas would be a good place to start to recreate the gestalt of Vancouver in the sixties.

When I mention the community of writers, this is not to suggest that there were no battles. Writers have been known for their vitriolic speech habits perhaps since writing began; but in the earlier part of the sixties, differences in style, subject, and ideology seemed to take a place behind cooperation and interest in the range of ideas available. Later in the sixties, this became less apparent to me, but this is very hard to quantify or elucidate. We definitely lived, and still live, in a class-ridden city, rife with sexism, racism, and small and vast crimes being committed in the name of free enterprise; but it is also a city of extraordinary beauty – geographic, artistic, and social.

The writers and artists I met at readings and galleries, I would also meet at demonstrations and meetings. The library was a hub of informal cultural activity. Of course, I was in my early twenties and new to the city, so my impressions are probably much more extreme than if I had been much older or used to the city. But it seemed as if the beauty, the ideas, and feelings around me were woven into an amazing concert, which helped to buoy up the sense of community I felt when I met various people.

Squaring the Vowels:
On the Visual Poetry of
Judith Copithorne

In Conversation with Gary Barwin

2013

Gary Barwin: Like many of your visual poems, this piece[1] has an intense spiritual attentive quality to it, a kind of unpretentious mysterious quality, and a kind of joyful shout-out to the delight that one can experience with forms and expression ... how do you imagine reading this poem?

Judith Copithorne: What you have to say about the individual portions of this piece is gorgeous, and I am very impressed and honoured by this, but this is not quite how I was working in this piece as far as I remember. I was working in a more physical manner with the actual visual reactions to the various physical attributes of the piece. Not too much red, just a little bit of straightening here, and so forth. And so especially when working in such a nonliteral area, I am basically pretty intuitive, although if I attend to it, I can usually come up with conceptual referents. And also, in general, I would characterize my attention as being a combination of left- and right-brain attributes. In fact, a balance of these processes feels and seems to be important to me.

As to the first question, I can really only answer thank you to you and not much else. These pieces are all gifts. I have very little control over them; although I have strong feelings and ideas, the actual expression of them is thanks to things I really can't control. And maybe my usual inability to do things any other way may actually in itself be a boon, in that it forces me to depend on the kindnesses of the rest of the universe. But it makes it pretty fraught if anyone wants me to commit to producing anything. In fact, I simply don't agree to produce any actual visual poetry or

---

1   This image can be seen in colour at jacket2.org/commentary/squaring-vowels.

written creative work unless I actually have it already in hand, and I always only offer work that I have already produced. That way when I get something new on the page it is a delightful surprise.

And this piece that you chose really was a surprise to me when it was finished, which happened very quickly as I remember. Firstly, I have very seldom used colour in my work for a variety of reasons. But sometimes, especially since I have been using a computer program, I get grabbed by the excitement and richness of the colour available on it, just as I sometimes get swept away by the variety of fascinating "tools" available, although I only have a black-and-white printer, so I only get to see the colour onscreen. I quite often print up the colour pieces, which I have recently started doing, in black and white. If they work well in black and white, I feel less extravagant about them. I haven't tried to print this one in black and white, actually, and when I have finished with this interview, I will try this and see what the result is. I am afraid that it may not have as much contrast as it should have to work well in black and white, but it is always interesting to see.

And also, in answer to your questions, specifically about the piece "Squared Vowels," I should say that part of my project with this piece was simply to effectively fill the whole page, square the vowels and the piece as a whole, as I quite often don't do that.

This piece is a bit of an anomaly to me, as I have not used that form of composition, and as well, I hadn't much used the function on the computer that produced the outlining and modulating of the shapes and colours. And as I said, I have not usually used so much colour as I have used in these pieces that I have done in the last couple of months. So I had several quite happy surprises when I saw the final result of these actions.

I can't really imagine at this point orally "reading" this poem out loud. This may be because I haven't had time for a long time to work on oral expression or maybe it really just is visual. I think that if I had time to work on this, I might be able to expand it into the oral realm. I sometimes do read some of my visual poetry out loud when pressed, but it is always pretty surprising to me and it has been years since I felt as if I had any handle on that.

Now here I guess I should clarify the nature of my pieces on vowels. They do not usually have the same literalness or linguistic qualities for me as the pieces I do that are built out of, or around, or with linear, linguistically derived language-oriented or even literal and transparent word-formed writing. Usually, I simply let the vowels be either sound pieces or, more often, abstract visual objects to be worked with as that.

So what I was involved with here was likely a simple combining of vowel shapes into what would hopefully become an interesting gestalt. And here, as elsewhere, the operation of chance was a huge motivator for me. Here I was mainly, I think, learning about how I could make these various "layers" (each letter is a separate "layer") interact, work with each other without cutting across each other too much and so on. I have always been interested in "layers" – that is what the Illustrator program calls them and that seems a good word for them. I have always been interested in the layers of an onion, of clouds, of the skin and the mind. These words and ideas, which may appear at first to be quite simple, are actually gigantic in their reverberations as words, as physical phenomena, as ideas, as physical and conceptual processes and visual representations or references, which can be fascinating, I find.

GB: You've been involved with visual poetry since the sixties. How do you think it has changed – not only the work itself, but its place in literature and in the arts in general? How would you say your work has evolved over time?

JC: I started imagining how to combine visual and written work pretty early on. I loved the illuminated pages from the *Book of Kells* that relatives sent at Christmas. And I wished to have the skills to produce political posters, as I felt strongly about some of the problems in the fifties, and posters seemed a possibility for dealing with the frustrations and pain that the McCarthy era and other parts of the surround too various to mention were producing. I also had a chance to see some of the [Russian] Constructivist work from the early twenties, although before the internet, this sort of material was much harder to access. Then around 1961, I got to visit City Lights bookstore and saw a small amount of some work by Henri Michaux and Brion Gysin.

So, I had been given a lot of clues, but there seemed to be a quite strong feeling at that time here in Vancouver that to do anything that might represent – that might seem to be disordered was at least a foolish thing to do and perhaps crazy or at least not "proper" and perhaps even "bad." I don't know how far to go in talking about this. There is so much that might be mentioned.

So yes, things have changed a lot and have moved towards a more open view of the possibilities of art and literature and life itself, although the forces of reaction and greed are also everywhere and physically getting more powerful and less ashamed of their own behaviour.

I am not sure that my work has actually changed that much, except that I have gradually become surer and clearer about what I want, or at least like, to do. The computer has certainly given me a huge amount more power and access, which I love, although in the end, *who* we are doesn't change that much, or so it seems. Not that I know much about any of this.

GB: Your work has always closely engaged with materials and the opportunities those materials inspire. Derek Beaulieu writes that your "suggestion that [your] pieces are drawn and not written and are hyphenated poem-drawings speaks to a textual hybridity which places looking on the same plane as reading." And more recently, you have been using computers, and so I think about the digital drawing and manipulations that you do in relationship to "drawing" vs. "writing" How do you conceive of the difference between drawing and writing, reading, and looking? Does the computer change this?

JC: The statement that, "Your work has always closely engaged with materials and the opportunities those materials inspire" is such an excellent statement to start off with, although I won't be specifically answering it, except to say that when I learned about art and literature in the fifties, that was supposed to be a very important approach to making artistic or literary work.

Having been so interested in the interface of the verbal and the visual since the fifties, ten years before I knew there was such a thing as concrete poetry, has perhaps made it easier for me to work in a variety of mediums which can be much more difficult for people today [particularly] if they have learned about these ideas, especially in schools which were more prescriptive than descriptive or experimental. But then sometimes such people will produce very clean, clear, and tight work which is well worth studying. And at the other end of the spectrum, there are also some brilliant, wide-seeing, and wild innovators working today, some of whom started quite recently. And then there are others of this grouping who have been around for what seems to me to have been a long time.

So perhaps what you originally know, and when you start, isn't so likely to direct you as your inborn disposition. However, this [could be so] if you conceptualize a whole range of existence being made up both of inert substances and then also energy – from the deep sleep range of one or two hertz per second up to beta waves at sixteen hertz per second through the speed of light waves, X-rays, gamma rays, the speeds of electrons and photons, and even up beyond that to that which we have not been able to visualize the extent of – then many shifts of thinking and perceiving become easier to entertain.

And then there is the perception that [we] detect and respond to literary material in a variety of places in the brain, most of which are fairly removed (as space in the brain might be considered) from where the brain processes visual perception. But it isn't completely cut and dried. Sometimes when one part of the brain is damaged, another part has been known to take over.

Then there are the cases of people with various forms of synesthesia. And then there are the times when people are scanning a "transparent" document, that is to say, a very literal and fascinating story, for example, and at those times, they will quite often hold in their minds images sometimes in a similar form to how we are sometimes aware of a dream for a short time after we wake up.

This then could be seen as an example of visual perception which occurs due to stimulus in the language-oriented parts of the brain. We speak of "conceptualization," but we haven't yet identified the actual nature of the physiological events which occur through the medium of the mind, brain, hand, and finger movements of a draftsperson or collagist or through the lips of a sound poet although such people as jwcurry or Gustave Morin are working on this.

And when I say a draftsperson, I am also referring to those people who may be drawing on a computer. Thus, much of this is another attempt to point out some of the multiple bases of "textual-hybridity," mixed media, working in several media at once or concurrently, and/or interdisciplinary collage, which was quite common in the twentieth century and has become more so in the twenty-first century.

And then there is the rise of digital media, particularly in the last twenty years, which has given rise to more ways to think about this. So basically, to skip the next three pages of my answers to your questions, I will answer that generally I find that the computer is a great boon and an economic annoyance. And in fact, I find that all media have similar good and bad sides.

GB: Much of your work was published in small press editions distributed to a number of artistic communities. Your work now frequently appears online (via Facebook, Flickr, as well as in online publications.) How do you think of community and publishing in terms of readers and fellow artists these days?

JC: [To] answer about communities of art and literature, particularly in regard to the computer, I guess my answer would be similar [to my last response]. *Homo sapiens* is an extremely mutable species. So adaptation is not particularly unusual. Whether I interact by mail, phone, face-to-face, or on the computer doesn't seem to make a huge amount of difference in the end.

I do feel that the community of people interested in visual poetry, surprising writing, experimentation in art and literature, and in general discovering what is possible in order to open out the world of the mind and support the needs of the world is growing and it feeds me. I worry about some health concerns, our very precarious political and environmental situation, getting old, and having to find another place to live when rents are so high, but I also feel support from some very important places, including the very kind and generous interest of this community.

It is very important to me to have people to talk to. It would be lovely if we all lived nearer to each other, but comprehension, attention, intelligence, and support are each made up primarily of non-physical things and they can be transmitted by letter, magazine, email, phone, and book as well as by face-to-face contact. And it seems that life goes by very, very fast, and the faster it goes, the less boring it gets. So this visual poetry activity I started doing back in 1961 has turned out to be an entry into a very exciting world.

And I also wanted to add that what I like best about visual poetry are the possibilities in it for surprise. I like literary and artistic speculation. I want to speculate on ideas rather than on land. I'd like creative endeavours to be our future instead of fracked gas. I like all kinds of visual and concrete poetry and many other kinds of art and literature, but what I like best is seeing something that surprises me in a way that opens up hopefully satisfactory possibilities, even if only to a small extent.

Surprising Writing

2018

primarily linguistic, kinetic, multidisciplined, intermedial, body-
oriented, mentally contrived, conceptual, cognitive, handworked,
eye created, typewritten, made with pen, created by breath,
by movable type, paper plate, stone, computer, printing press,
silkscreen, collage, hypothalamus, foot, eye, Letraset, ear, syllable,
metre, word, beat, photocopy, line, iPhone, brush, the possibilities
are as multiple as the uses of paper, wood, papyrus, film, screen,
& so forth (& for further complexity, don't forget inscription on
some bacteria).

once we had three dimensions, or four really. then physicists started
to investigate the spheres of the subatomic & outer space & found
three more dimensions. so why wouldn't poetry have a few more
ways of looking, listening, & exploring?

we started doing concrete poetry here in Vancouver fifty years
ago, before anyone else around here was doing it & almost before
anyone else in Canada. the idea then was that of opening the
borders of the page which was tremendously exciting. as far as we
knew very few had gone beyond the parameters & margins of the
poetry which was available to us. what the young or those who are
otherwise uninitiated are often told is that first you have to learn all
there is to learn about a subject & then you are ready to produce
some new ideas. but somehow, this time, the world got there ahead
of the rule books & took us with it.

for well over ten thousand years people have been drawing &
singing & not long after that they started writing. they have done all
of these things in whatever way it was possible for them to do them
at that particular moment using whatever technologies & materials
were available. the idea that there are certain ways art or poetry
must be made is of use if you wish to describe these ways but often
it doesn't open up new & innovative ways of thinking or being
& of producing new & interesting work. rules can be as much an
anathema as a support to innovation, speculation, & variety.

curiosity, interest, expectation, disconcertion, speculation, shock, expansion, jolt, are some experiences in a beholder a concrete poem hopefully might occasion.

for me that is still one of the most interesting things about concrete poetry. for such poetry doesn't stay where you put it. it starts moving around on the page, in the mind, on the screen, in the dirt. wherever it starts it has vitality & imagination. concrete poetry can often be politically involved, riotous, careful, extravagant, meticulous, exquisite, & sadly, sometimes it is mundane & pedestrian. but to me, the time when it's most interesting & perhaps when one of its most interesting purposes is realized is when it is surprising, unexpected, & outside the bounds.

PART TWO: INCLUSIVE WRITING

1. much of life concerns areas we usually avoid thinking about, such as bodily functions, our debts, old age, & our various fears, rational & otherwise. and often we characterize these as being part of our unconscious & try to leave them there unseen. but frequently our "unconscious" appears to eventually make these subjects visible in ways we have difficulty controlling or which we actually cannot control.

2. in regard to what we can or cannot & do or do not control it might be useful to regard the fact that quite often people comment on how there are so few women doing concrete poetry, but if you start to look at what is being seen today compared with what was seen in 1960 you would notice that there are many more women to be seen today in this field than there were then. so "things" have changed to some degree in this area although they have certainly not changed that much yet.

3. as I hope will become clear there are a couple of differing but related sets of arguments going here at the same time. P. Coelho said: "if you think adventure is dangerous, try routine; it is lethal."

& that is to some degree what this is trying to say. this may not be capable of producing adventure but perhaps it will move in the direction of looking at concrete poetry as a field which may open some further possibilities.

4. in 1968 Intermedia had perhaps at one time or another four hundred people actively participating in its creation in a manner that was more or less involved with avoiding hierarchical activities. & Intermedia was more or less based on Motion Studio, which was active in 1966 & which had (more or less) 150 active participants. & Motion Studio was based on the Sound Gallery which had more or less fifteen active creators & many other participants. & the Sound Gallery was mainly based on Al Neil's music & sculpture & Helen Goodwin's creative dance activities. both of these people were working in their fields here in Vancouver before 1960. so it is pretty hard to pin down when these forms of experimental art entered Vancouver, or anywhere else, but obviously it was before 1960. although it is questionable that timelines are that important in the making of concrete poetry. what is important, to me, is the state of one's mind & one's life as a whole. a sense of humour really helps too.

5. there were so many people in that experimental sphere who were very important to it, such as Al Neil, Helen Goodwin, Sam Perry, Gregg Simpson, bill bissett, Gary Lee-Nova, Ken Ryan. these people were paramount to these various ventures & many other people were too. thus some sorts of inclusiveness become important just to iterate the numbers of people involved. & in concrete poetry the same situation existed & continues to exist. some people function as prisms, they focus light or insight or energy & yet usually without a broad base of interested people not a lot is likely to happen. who these people are & what their interest is is another whole story which even my attempts at inclusiveness cannot contain here.

6. there are two ways to analyze such activities as these, the inclusive & the exclusive. & of course things are never completely exclusive or inclusive but for convenience this piece, from now on, will speak in these terms. of all of these activities, most of the people I have talked to, & certainly I, have maintained the impression that a primarily inclusive view of Intermedia, concrete poetry, & many other individual & group activities & events, particularly from the "sixties," was &, I am arguing, is still useful. this was a time of, to paraphrase McLuhan, the medium being the message & the message in all of this was the interaction of ideas & media &, as E.M. Forster pointed out in *Howards End*, the importance of remembering to "Only connect."

7. for now there seems little point in talking for too long about the past. so to go on, I was asked recently what I would do (for example) when concrete poetry was to be discussed. & I would now say that it appears that it is important to allow people more time for moving around & maybe getting into smaller groups & having more immediate interchanges. to me the possibilities of concrete & sound poetry & other newer forms are about just that, possibilities, immediacy, avoiding what is set & under control. yet it is often difficult for people to do this at the start. people often need to attempt to stretch themselves mentally & socially in order to become more flexible so they can relax enough to think & act in more varied ways (without just falling apart or trying to take over) or, on the other hand, ending up feeling socially compromised, bored, or powerless & the fear of powerlessness, it should be noted, is an extremely strong & often quite unconscious motive for some people.

8. thus there are questions I could ask of the present attempts to create definitive, critical analyses of concrete poetry. for to me these are very interesting projects which unfortunately may be headed, to some degree, on several levels, towards certain kinds of misrepresentation unless they take into account the complexities & some of the, until now, often apparently undetected but important characteristics of this field.

PART THREE: GENERATIVE WRITING

1. a brilliant interface of the visual & verbal was first made public in Brazil around 1955.[1] Both before & after this, other forms of visual & verbal combinations have made their presence known. Among the names that some of this work has been given are visual poetry & vispo. Here several other names are being suggested, such as Inclusive, Multidisciplinary, & Generative Poetry (or Writing).

2. Most concrete & visual poetry & vispo (& it is being proposed, although some may disagree, that these names, although representing a variety of special forms & ideas, are quite often similar enough to be used here somewhat interchangeably) is usually made on some form of two-dimensional surface of a size that is easily perceived at one time. From cave wall to map, from papyrus to screen, a similar two-dimensional model has been common across cultures. The figures on this surface may be "read" according to the direction that the writing in that culture moves, but that is not always the case & the direction the eye is led in may be quite varied. And the material presented has been probably as varied as the spread of human sensation, emotion, conceptualization, & perception. Visual poetry has taken its form from multiple aspects of our lives. Some is formed of an emptiness or irony, which may make us aware of the vacuous nature of capitalism. Other forms invite involvement with combinations of visual, verbal, or auditory wit or exposition & with sensual, emotive, or intellectual "images" in the brain, body, or nervous system. Beauty's doubts & variety, curiosity & anger are other combinatory forces which may generate or be generated by this writing.

---

1   The 1950s were a significant period for the international emergence of concrete poetry, including the formation of the Brazilian Noigandres group. The group consisted of Décio Pignatari, Haroldo de Campos, and Augusto de Campos. [Editor's note].

3. It appears that people have been writing, drawing, & singing
    at least since they started leaving remnants of their activities
    on the earth. They appear to have done this in whatever way it
    was possible for them to do so at that particular moment using
    whatever technologies (materials & methods) were available. The
    idea that there are only certain ways to make art or poetry may
    be of use if you wish to describe these ways, but it doesn't always
    make it possible to expand or refine previous work or to open up
    new or more varied or fruitful ways of producing further work.

4. For me that is still the most interesting thing about concrete or
    visual poetry. This is poetry that doesn't stay where you put it.
    It starts moving around on the page, in the mind, on the screen,
    in the dirt. Wherever it starts it has vitality, imagination. It is
    speculative, it grows. Speculation differs greatly from proof. Proof
    is for such activities as those of doing science, mathematics, &
    commerce & sometimes, these days, even physical proof is no
    longer a necessary accompaniment to acceptance in some forms
    of physics at least. So proof would probably not be a necessary
    characteristic of literary or artistic form.

5. Recent discoveries using fMRI, EEG, & other brain imaging have
    produced so much information on how our brains work that older
    theories of psychology sometimes appear to be disappearing
    beneath this gigantic quantity of data. And until the staggering
    complexity of each organism is considered it makes little sense that
    so much could be discovered using each of these views. But when
    we stop to think of the many billions of cells which comprise each
    person the intricacy of the ideas emerging to describe our world
    begins to be understandable.

6. This universe is so large & complex that it appears not to be possible for us, at this point, to comprehend either its final size or nature. So why would we wish to close off our attempts to examine it using whatever means are available to each of us? And writing & poetry, to name a couple possible disciplines, are part of the many possible methods which can be used for this examination.

7. On the walls of caves we see brilliant depictions of people hunting, dancing, moving & each is portrayed using the slightest of equipment & signs. At the topmost edges of maps we see the four winds. Much, including philosophy, love, anger, gesture, political will, rhythm, musical notation has been translated or reproduced on pages of concrete or visual poetry.

8. It appears that conscious activity is almost always multiconceptual. Overriding waves of emotion, idea, or sensation which can be measured in range of around sixty hertz per second, which is well above the usual focus, or beta waves of sixteen to twenty hertz, may bind the multiple concepts operating at one time & create greater energy, but unless that larger outline includes further consciousness of the varied impulses operating within its purview the result of this new energetic activity will be unable to go beyond the confines of its own nature. Since recent research suggests that the human brain is apparently bent towards conceptual blending, an awareness of this inherent activity will help to clarify, for example, the power of images when combined with language.

Editor's Note

All works selected for *Another Order* are previously published works by Judith Copithorne, featured in print and online between the years 1965 and 2019, including full-length books, chapbooks, and other kinds of literary ephemera. No periodical publications have been included except for short essays and an interview. Every effort has been made to select from as many works as possible but, given the ephemeral nature of small-press production, some texts remain elusive. In some cases, texts from Copithorne's oeuvre have been excerpted to meet the requirements of the publisher or, in other cases, they were not included if they have been reprinted as standalone works or as revised versions in other collections. Page order in *Phases / Phrases* has been altered to enable printing of colour images. Small emendations and alterations have been made to some of the texts when possible to correct spelling as requested by the author, to update the language, and in other cases to meet the Talonbooks house style. Texts in this selection whose titles begin with "from …" have been excerpted. It is worth noting, too, that *Heart's Tide* had been excerpted to meet the publisher's page limitations. A […] in the text indicates that only a part of that entry has been included. Interested readers are encouraged to seek out *Heart's Tide* in its original published form to see the full text. The definition for bracket on page 188, included as part of *Brackets & Boundaries*, was taken verbatim from Eric Partridge's *Origins: A Short Etymological Dictionary of Modern English* (1988). With few exceptions, all visual, concrete, and hybrid works have been digitally scanned by the editor and carefully prepared for publication by Leslie Smith at Talonbooks. Given the idiosyncratic nature of small-press production, some of the visual works have been resized to fit the publication format or, where necessary, edited to enhance colour or clarity. Some of the striking material qualities – paper, binding, stitching, etc. – of Copithorne's original publications are lost in the movement of texts from the first edition to this selected edition. Readers of this edition, for example, will not see the skillful craft that characterizes many of the first edition small runs. Enthusiastic readers are encouraged to seek opportunities to see first editions of these works to enjoy the original productions but should know that Copithorne's writing and drawing are centred here over the fine material and paratextual details.

Publications included or drawn from for this volume include *Returning* (1965), *Meandering* (1967), *Where Have I Been?* (1967), *Rain* (1969), *Release* (1969), *Runes* (1970), *Miss Tree's Pillow Book* (1971), *Until Now* (1971), *Heart's Tide* (1972), *Arrangements* (1973), *Albion's Rose Blooms to Calypso Beat* (1985), *A Light Character* (1985), *Horizon* (1992), the *Capilano Review* (1997), the *Vancouver Sun* (2008), *Making Waves: Reading BC and Pacific Northwest Literature* (2010), *Brackets & Boundaries {Concrete & Other Accretions}* (2011), *Surprising Writing* (2012), *Jacket2* (2013), and *Phases / Phrases* (2019).

Selected Bibliography

WORKS BY JUDITH COPITHORNE

Returning. Vancouver: Returning Press, 1965.

Meandering. Vancouver: Returning Press, 1967.

Where Have I Been? Vancouver: Very Stone House, 1967.

Winter Song. Vancouver: privately published, 1968.

Release. Vancouver: Bau-Xi Gallery, 1969.

Rain. Toronto: Ganglia Press, 1969.

And Blood Poured Down. Vancouver: privately published, 1970.

Runes. Toronto/Vancouver: Coach House/Intermedia Press, 1970.

A Tree as Always. Vancouver: Ace Space, 1971.

Colour Song. Vancouver: privately published, 1971.

Fire Flowers. Vancouver: privately published, 1971.

Miss Tree's Pillow Book. Vancouver: Intermedia Press, 1971.

Natural Events. Vancouver: privately published, 1971.

Heart's Tide. Vancouver: privately published, 1971.

Kaliyuga. Vancouver: Intermedia Press, n.d. [ca. 1970].

Heart's Tide. 2nd ed. Vancouver: Vancouver Community Press, 1972.

History's Wife: A Sculpture. Vancouver: Vancouver Cultural Feedback
        Project, 1972.

Arrangements. Vancouver: Intermedia Press, 1973.

Albion's Rose Blooms to Calypso Beat. Toronto: Ganglia Press, 1985.

A Light Character. Toronto: Coach House Press, 1985.

Third Day of Fast. Vancouver: Silver Birch Press, 1987.

2nd Thoughts. Vancouver: privately published, 1987.

I Tried So Hard to Make Some Art. Vancouver: privately published, 1990.

On Median: 8. Burnaby: Beaver Kosmos and West Coast Line, 1990.

Falling Behind. North Vancouver: Silver Birch Press, 1991.

Horizon. Toronto: Pangen Subway Ritual, 1992.

Carbon Dioxide. Vancouver: Silver Birch Press, 1992.

For My Ancestors. Toronto: Curvd H&z, 1994.

Tern. Vancouver: Returning Press, 2001.

Selections from 25 Hertz. Vancouver: privately published, 2003.

Erase. Ottawa: Curvd H&z, 2005.

Noniterative Enmity Reducing Venn Derivation. Ottawa: Curvd H&z, 2005.

Tithe. Ottawa: 1cent, 2005.

Redro. Ottawa: Curvd H&z, 2006.

Opposites. Ottawa: 1cent, 2007.

Brackets & Boundaries {Concrete & Other Accretions}. Vancouver: Returning Press, 2011.

Surprising Writing – Part 1. Calgary: No Press, 2012.

See Lex Ions. Lafarge, WI: Xerolage, 2015.

Surprising Writing. Vancouver: Retern Press, 2018.

"About Visual Poetry." *Utsanga*, March 27, 2018. www.utsanga.it/copithorne -about-visual-petry/.

Phases / Phrases. British Columbia: Trainwreck Press, 2019.

EDITED BY JUDITH COPITHORNE

Returning Press One. Vancouver: Returning Press, 1972.

Returning Two. Vancouver: Returning Press, 1972.

Return : Three. Vancouver: Returning Press, 1973.

ANTHOLOGIES FEATURING WORK BY JUDITH COPITHORNE

west coast seen. Edited by Jim Brown. Vancouver: Talonbooks, 1969.

The Cosmic Chef. Edited by bpNichol. Ottawa: Oberon Press, 1970.

I Am a Sensation. Edited by Gerry Goldberg and George Wright. Toronto: McClelland & Stewart, 1971.

New Direction in Canadian Poetry. Edited by John Robert Colombo. Toronto/ Montreal: Holt, Rinehart, and Winston, 1971.

Four Parts Sand. Edited by Michael Macklem. Ottawa: Oberon Press, 1972.

where? the other canadian poetry. Edited by Eldon Garnet. Erin, ON: Press Porcepic, 1974.

THE LAST BLEWOINTMENT ANTHOLOGY VOLUME I. Edited by bill bissett. Toronto: Nightwood Editions, 1985.

Vancouver Poetry. Edited by Allan Safarik. Winlaw, BC: Polestar Press, 1986.

radiant danse uv being: a poetic portrait of bill bissett. Roberts Creek, BC: Nightwood Editions, 2006.

Force Field. Edited by Susan Musgrave. Salt Spring Island, BC: Mother Tongue Publishing, 2008.

Making Waves: Reading B.C. and Pacific Northwest Literature. Edited by Trevor Carolan. Vancouver: Anvil Press; Abbotsford: UFV Press, 2010.

The Last Vispo Anthology: Visual Poetry, 1998–2000. Edited by Crag Hill and Nico Vassilakis. Seattle: Fantagraphics, 2012.

The New Concrete: Visual Poetry in the 21st Century. Edited by Victoria Bean and Chris McCabe. London: Hayward Gallery Publishing, 2015.

Judith: Women Making Visual Poetry. Edited by Amanda Earl. Malmö, Sweden: 2021.

SELECTED CRITICISM AND MENTIONS

Bayard, Caroline. *The New Poetics in Canada and Quebec: From Concretism to Post-Modernism.* Toronto: University of Toronto Press, 1989.

Beaulieu, Derek. "Abstract / Concrete #1: Judith Copithorne." *Lemon Hound.* December 12, 2012.

Betts, Gregory. "A Line, A New Line, All One: Variant Narratives of Concrete Canada." In *Finding Nothing: The VanGardes, 1959–1975,* 179–213. Toronto: University of Toronto Press, 2021.

———. "Postmodern Decadence in Sound and Visual Poetry." In *RE: Reading the Postmodern,* edited by Robert David Stacey, 151–179. Ottawa: University of Ottawa Press, 2010.

———. "Theory of the Avant-Gardes in Canada." In *Avant-Garde Canadian Literature: The Early Manifestations,* 26–85. Toronto: University of Toronto Press, 2013.

Brown, Lorna. "GLUT: Beginning with Language." In *Beginning with the Seventies,* 33–53. Vancouver: Morris and Helen Belkin Art Gallery and Information Office, 2020.

Butling, Pauline. "bpNichol and a Gift Economy: The Play of Value and the Value of Play." In *Writing in Our Time: Canada's Radical Poetries in English (1957–2003),* edited by Pauline Butling and Susan Rudy, 61–78. Waterloo: Wilfrid Laurier University Press, 2005.

———. "*Tish*: 'The Problem of Margins.'" In *Writing in Our Time: Canada's Radical Poetries in English (1957–2003),* edited by Pauline Butling and Susan Rudy, 49–60. Waterloo: Wilfrid Laurier University Press, 2005.

"Copithorne, Judith." *ABC Bookworld.* 2012. abcbookworld.com/writer /copithorne-judith/.

curry, jw. "proof no burden: a start at a Judith Copithorne checklist." *1cent* 400 and *Newsnotes* 13 (March 15, 2009): unpaginated.

Davey, Frank. "Poetry beyond Illocution." *Studies in Canadian Literature / Études en littérature canadienne* 41, no. 1 (December 1, 2016): 162–81, journals.lib.unb.ca/index.php/SCL/article/view/25423.

Earl, Amanda. "Introduction: This Book Is an Action." In *Judith: Women Making Visual Poetry,* edited by Amanda Earl, 18–25. Malmö, Sweden: Timglaset Editions, 2021.

———. "Women at the Vanguard of Visual Poetry, If Only We Had Known:

Overcoming Erasure to Make Connections between Past, Present, and Future Women Making Visual Poetry." *Periodicities: A Journal of Poetry and Poetics*, March 23, 2021. periodicityjournal.blogspot.com/2021/03 /amanda-earl-women-at-vanguard-of-visual.html.

Emerson, Lori. "women dirty concrete poets." *loriemerson – dot net* (blog), May 4, 2011. loriemerson.net/2011/05/04/women-dirty-concrete-poets/.

Gerson, Carole, and Yvan Lamonde. "Books and Reading in Canadian Art." In *History of the Book in Canada. Vol. 3, 1918–1980,* edited by Carole Gerson and Jacques Michon, 75–80. Toronto: University of Toronto Press, 2007.

Leduc, Natalie. "Concrete Poetry: R u p t u r i n g the Modes of Doing Poetry." Chap. 1 in *"Dissensus and Poetry: The Poet as Activist in Experimental English-Canadian Poetry."* Master's thesis, University of Ottawa, 2019, 15–48. dx.doi.org/10.20381/ruor-23025.

mclennan, rob. *"Judith: Women Making Visual Poetry,* ed. Amanda Earl." *rob mclennan's blog,* July 1, 2021. robmclennan.blogspot.com/2021/07/judith -women-making-visual-poetry-ed.html.

Schmaltz, Eric. "'my body of bliss': Judith Copithorne's Concrete Poetry in the 1960s and 1970s." *Canadian Poetry* 83 (Fall–Winter 2018): 14–39, canadianpoetry.org/wp-content/uploads/2020/03/Studies-1-83.pdf.

———. *Borderblur Poetics: Intermedia and Avant-Gardism in Canada, 1963–1988.* Calgary: University of Calgary Press, 2023.

Schofield, Anakana. "Concrete Vancouver." Anakana Schofield (website), March 9, 2010. anakanaschofield.com/2010/03/09/1240/.

"Squaring the Vowels: On the Visual Poetry of Judith Copithorne." Interview by Gary Barwin. *Jacket2,* October 23, 2013. jacket2.org/commentary /squaring-vowels.

Tallman, Warren. "Wonder Merchants: Modernist Poetry in Vancouver during the 1960's." *Boundary 2,* vol. 3, no. 1 (Autumn 1974): 57–90, doi.org/10.2307 /302408.

Turner, Michael. "Expanded Literary Practices." Ruins in Process: Vancouver Art in the Sixties (website). Morris and Helen Belkin Art Gallery, the University of British Columbia, and grunt gallery. expandedliterarypractices.vancouverartinthesixties.com/.

Whistle, Ian. "Ian Whistle on Judith Copithorne." *many gendered mothers* (blog), April 17, 2017. themanygenderedmothers.blogspot.com/2017/04 /ian-whistle-on-judith-copithorne.html.

Acknowledgments

With the deepest gratitude, the editor would like to thank the following people whose various forms of support, enthusiasm, and friendship assisted in the completion of this edition: Stephen Cain for his friendship and support as this work grew from conversation to collection; Karis Shearer, Deanna Fong, and Jordan Abel for helping this project find a home with Talonbooks; additional thanks to Deanna for sharing project-related material; Catriona Strang, Kevin Williams, and Leslie Smith of Talonbooks for seeing this project through; Ryan Fitzpatrick for his proofreading prowess; Gregory Betts and Derek Beaulieu for support, enthusiasm, and resource sharing; Teresa Sudeyko at the Morris and Helen Belkin Art Gallery for correspondence and resource sharing; Shannon Maguire, who offered me space to share the first iteration of a paper that would grow into larger ideas about the works collected here; Stephen Remus and Natasha Pedros of the Niagara Artists Centre for facilitating a first opportunity to work with Judith in a gallery setting; D.M.R. Bentley and *Canadian Poetry: Studies, Documents, Reviews* for offering a first home to some of the ideas in this collection's introduction; James Macdonald at The Printed Word, jwcurry at Room 302 Books, Jay Millar at Apollinaire's Bookshoppe, Charles Purpora at Purpora Books, and Bastion Books for giving refuge to important and often overlooked books of avant-garde literature; Gregg Simpson for sharing his memories of Judith in Vancouver; John Shoesmith at the Thomas Fisher Special Collections at the University of Toronto for his assistance in locating materials; the staff at St. Jude's Anglican Home for their kindness and support; Robert Copithorne and Adrienne Copithorne for their encouragement and commitment to this project; Renee Rodin and Ron Janssen for their enthusiasm and support of this project; Joseph Ianni for loaning me books that I did not know I needed; Robert Anderson for equipment advice; Kate Siklosi, Aaron Kreuter, Myra Bloom, Phil Miletic, and Greg Fast for conversation and friendship; Alysha Dawn Puopolo always, for her love and support, for being a positive force in my life.

Born in Vancouver in 1939 to an artistic family, **Judith Copithorne** is a poet, writer, and artist who has made many notable contributions to concrete poetry and other intermedia contexts from the 1960s through to the present. In the 1960s and 1970s, she was identified as an affiliate of Vancouver's so-called Downtown Poets and was involved with Vancouver's alternative art venues, including Sound Gallery, Motion Studio, and Intermedia. She was published in the first issues of *blewointment* and *Ganglia* and continues to publish her work today through small or private presses. Her work has been anthologized in *New Direction in Canadian Poetry* (1971), *The Cosmic Chef* (1970), *Four Parts Sand* (1972), *THE LAST BLEWOINTMENT ANTHOLOGY VOLUME 1* (1985), *The Last Vispo Anthology: Visual Poetry, 1998–2008* (2012), and *Judith: Women Making Visual Poetry* (2021), among other places. Lifting her work off the page, she has been featured in numerous gallery exhibitions, including the *Concrete Poetry Festival* (1969), *Microprosophus* (1971), *The Bird is the Word* (2011), *Beginning with the Seventies: GLUT* (2018), and *Concrete Is Porous* (2018–2020). Her work is widely influential for multiple generations of poets living and working today.

Eric Schmaltz is the author of *Borderblur Poetics: Intermedia and Avant-Gardism in Canada, 1963–1988* (University of Calgary Press) and co-editor of *I Want to Tell You Love* by bill bissett and Milton Acorn (University of Calgary Press). He is also the author of the poetry book *Surfaces* (Invisible Publishing) and several shorter intermedial works, published by national and international small presses. He holds a Ph.D. in English from York University and was a Social Sciences and Humanities Research Council Post-doctoral Fellow in the English Department at the University of Pennsylvania. He lives in Tkaronto (Toronto), where he teaches creative writing and Canadian literature and works as Writer-on-the-Grounds at York University's Glendon College.

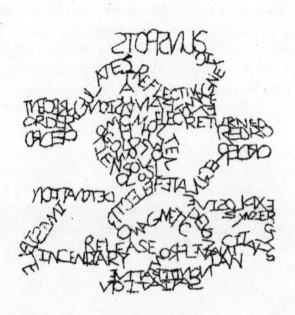